Society And The Computing Power

<u>Sadie Miriam</u>

1

Table of Contents

How is information created & where does it come from?

It is said that one finds the meaning of a word in its source.

It's clear that there are many different opinions about what information is & where & how it's created.

My doxie comes mostly from information theory.

I've been at the Massachusetts Institute of Technology (MIT) for many years now, where information theory was founded & where it's still discussed.

The answer to all these questions is: no

For example, what is the information content of the sentence "It is raining."? If we can measure it, say in bits, are we dealing with an information content of 50 bits or three bits? Or does it depend on whether we represent the sentence in ASCII or some other binary code? It's just that this message, that is, the sentence "It's raining." in itself has no meaning at all. The question of how much information a message has is simply a wrongly asked question. It cannot be answered. What do I mean? It's pretty simple. We have a source of the message. I'd rather speak of a message than information. Because that's not the same thing. & we have a channel through which the message is transmitted to a recipient.

Information theory has various tasks. For example, it deals with how many signals can be transmitted over a certain channel in a certain time. A question of information theory is how to recover the correct bit string when the signal series or bit string being transmitted over the channel is corrupted. Engineers know that the channel is never flawless. There is a noise. & so the question arises as to how, despite this noise, the message can be sent in such a way that it arrives correctly.

A question that does not arise at all in information theory is what a given bit string means. Here is an example by Warren Weaver, written in *Scientific American* around 1946 or 1947 . At that time people in America still drove trains. It was about a lawyer in New York who was dealing with a deal in Chicago. So he had to drive back & forth more often. One day he said to his wife, "I have to go back to Chicago tomorrow. Of course I'll take the Empire State Express from New York to Chicago & back again. I think the contract will work."

completed on Thursday, so I'll be back Thursday evening. Holmich at Grand Central Station, the train always arrives at the same time.'

The lawyer's wife got his telegram on Tuesday. & it went something like this: »My dear Susi. We got the deal a lot sooner than we thought, so I'm going to take the Empire State Express back tonight. Please pick me up at Grand Central Station at 5 p.m. I love you, your Karl.' The question that arises is: How much information did the lawyer send? He writes 'My dear Susi', but it would be sufficient to say: 'Susi'. Or he can omit the name altogether, since the telegram was sent to her. & then: "The contract was signed much earlier than we thought, so I'm going back tonight on the Empire State Express." Of course, if he's back on Tuesday evening, then that must mean the contract has already been signed. That's all done, so he can get out of Chicago. Since he always takes the Empire State Express, he might as well skip that. She also already knows that the train is arriving at Grand Central Station & what time the train is arriving. It's also nice of him to say he loves her, but she already knows that. This isn't new news to her. So it would be sufficient if he sent her an empty telegram. Then she would already know what this means.

Now, can we say that the information in this message is a bit? No, we can't. Maybe he's a communist & the FBI reads his correspondence. It may believe that there is a secret message hidden in the telegram. The relevant people are given the telegram for analysis & want to investigate its meaning. What does that tell us? It tells us that the meaning of a message depends on the recipient's state, or

more precisely, of its expected state. The receiver interprets the message in a certain way in the light of this state. So the magic word is interpretation.

The objection could be raised here that the person receiving a telegram would like some confirmation of what is actually intended. But the lawyer's wife knows exactly what to do. She goes into Grand Central Station, & at Platform 32 the Empire State Express from Chicago arrives at a specific time. It may very well be that what the attorney was trying to say, the information that is trying to induce in the recipient, isn't as simple as that. The fact that he writes "I love you" could mean, for example:

"I'm coming with my girlfriend & it would be better if you didn't pick me up." We don't know. & that's exactly what I mean; the message has to do with the state & especially with the expected state of the recipient.

How is information generated? Where is information generated? Where does information come from? I now look away from the animals & say: There is only one source & that is the living man. A message I receive, or rather the signals I receive e.g. B. on the television, over the phone, in a conversation or through body language, I transform it into information by interpreting it. Interpretation is the work that has to be done in order, for example, to convert a message, a signal string or a bit string into information.

Is information a relationship? No she is not. information is produced. We produce information by hearing or seeing signals, for example, by receiving them & then interpreting them. We may or may not interpret them correctly. But what does correct mean? This has to do with the intention of the sender. I can imagine saying something to someone & believing that I will be understood.

This means that the receiver interprets what is said correctly, in the same way that I would interpret it. That is correctness. But I cannot know that.

A good question seems to me to be how is it possible that we understand each other at all when we exchange signals. Body language is sometimes very difficult to interpret & can also be very easily misinterpreted.

We can understand each other as we have been socialized in the same culture. This socialization has given us the technology we use to interpret signals. It's very different in another culture. I would like to give you an example: I was in Japan & one evening a family invited me to their house. This is a high honor in Japan. The father sat down & said he had a problem with his son. Since I knew the world & was much older, he wanted to tell me the problem & get my advice. Eventually I told him that the difference between his & my socialization was so big that I could repeat his problem but not really understand it. Therefore I could I him, or rather: therefore I should not give him an answer.

Similarly with the computer: we might be able to create an artificial intelligence system that would be used in the judiciary. & the computer decides what to do with a delinquent. I'm not even talking about whether that's possible or not. But I do know one thing: we shouldn't do it because the computer's algorithms can't take the cultural aspects of our society into account. The computer cannot understand this. But people actually work on stuff like that. They say, for example, in America:

One thing is for sure, the computer is color blind. So when a black man & a white man are judged by the computer, the computer doesn't even notice that one is black & the other is black

the other knows. So is the computer more objective? Nonsense! Also, the judge may be absolutely right in recognizing & taking into account the color of the defendant's skin as more important in the given case.

We speak of the computer as an information processing machine. But that is not the case. The computer processes signals that are absolutely meaningless to it.

Thecomputercontainsnoinformationinthe ensethatbitstringshaveanymeaningtothecom puter.Theyareabsolutelymeaningless.Thesear esignalsthataretransmitted. When we say that the computer tells us it will rain tomorrow, we mean that we interpret what the computer shows us on the screen or on the printer or wherever as a prediction that it will rain tomorrow. But the computer doesn't know that it's going to rain. If we have a weather simulation in the computer & it rains, then the computer won't get wet either. In a lecture on the DNA chain, Professor Hans Rosenthal said that if you know the complete DNA of a chicken, you know everything knows all there is to know about this animal. But one cannot conclude from this chain of signals that it is a chicken. This behaves very analogously to a computer. Let's imagine a simple computer, eg a laptop. Let's say I find a laptop. It is quite clear that it is working. You can see the small light of the control lamp, you can also hear the hard disk clicking. So he's running. I take the laptop to my lab & examine it with good instruments. After a while I know the state of the computer at a certain point in time, say in a certain microsecond. For this moment, I know the entire state of the computer, i.e. all its components & bit sequences

If you know all that, then you know absolutely everything you can possibly know about the computer. Now someone comes along & asks: "What does it calculate anyway?" We may be dealing with a word processor busy working on a manuscript. It may also be a stock computer calculating what stocks to buy tomorrow or the next minute. The computer may also be able to process pornographic images. I can't find out all of that. It's the same story as chicken DNA. If the computer were an information processing system, then I should be able to use my instruments to find out what information is being processed. But I can't do that.

We have high hopes for our technical

systems & especially for our so-called information systems. We speak of the information society. & people talk about the new instruments of the information society as if they would give us a whole new chance to strengthen democracy, to fight poverty, etc. In my opinion, that is a mistake. The problems our world is confronted with, I mean poverty, war, environmental disasters, etc., do not exist – to put it colloquially – because we lack certain information. It is an illusion to think that if we search the Internet we will find information that will help us solve such problems. A famous American philosopher, William Rogers, once said: It is not what we do not know that harms us. It is everything we know that is not true. We have political, human & social problems. But I think that in solving them, the power that we have gained through so-called information processing is simply irrelevant.

Information Highway & the Global Village

Data super highways & *information highways.* Let's try to find out what these metaphors mean. The word »autobahn« evokes two different associations in me. To my knowledge, the term first appeared in the German language during the Nazi era. Autobahns were first built in the 1930s, at least that's what I think, to combat unemployment in Germany. The second & perhaps even more important reason was to create a fast transport network for war supplies, so that military goods & soldiers could be transported more quickly from one place to another. For me, it is also remarkable that the idea of the Volkswagen in Germany & with it increasing prosperity was being propagated for broad sections of the population. Everyone should have a Volkswagen, so it was said.

The second term *information highway* has its origins around the beginning of the 1960s. In the USA, the aim was to develop a military communications network that would also work in times of war & even after a conceivable nuclear war. There were a lot of funny & sometimes crazy ideas & ideas in America at that time. For example, in the event of a nuclear explosion, it was often recommended to crawl quickly under a table or other cover, or if necessary

Hold a briefcase over your head during the detonation, trying to give the impression that this might help. In addition, one should build protective devices at home & take further precautions. Later, much later, came the idea of SDI, i.e. the plan of a protective shield & screen over North America to protect against a missile attack.

My experience with autobahns, not data autobahns, began around 1939 in America, when the first autobahn was to be built in Pennsylvania, following the example of German autobahns. It was said back then that it wouldn't be long before highways like this were built all over America, & that it would make driving from one coast to the other, north to south, & all over the world, much easier. In fact, that's how it happened. The traffic on the freeways has reached enormous proportions to this day, & not just to the benefit of mankind.

Let's think about what is happening in detail, what is actually whizzing by on these freeways, & I would like to use this as an analogy to a data superhighway. Well, cars are whizzing by over the freeways, more or less quickly, & in the case of the highways, data is whizzing by, you could say. & what whizzing down the information highway? That's my next question. The answer seems clear: information. But that's not true. Unfortunately, the word information is used incorrectly here. We should remember what we are actually talking about when we talk about information. What actually happens through computers, through the pathways & networks, these are signals or just data. Signals is perhaps the better word. We know signals at traffic lights or railway lines: red or green. The railways used to have simple signs that signaled either *stop* or *go* . The train driver knew what these signals mean. With the help of training & experience, he was able to recognize the signals.

who came towards him interpret. It is very important to distinguish this & to know how signals or simple data only become information through our knowledge, through experience & through interpretation.

I would like to explain this a bit more with the help of two small examples. I'll start with the slightly longer example. Let's say you have the Manhattan phone book in New York in front of you. Does that phone book contain a lot of information? My answer is: no. It's not full of information, it's full of data or signals. But I can get information from it. However, I have to actually produce that information first. In order for this to happen, in a sense, I have to have a hypothesis that will help me interpret the data that's in the phone book , tend to live together in one area & are not randomly scattered across the district. That's my hypothesis. I think I know that almost all Armenian surnames end in -ian, e.g. Agopian. Now I search the entire phone book using a computer, & every name I come across that ends with

-ianfind, write down the phone number or the corresponding zip code. If I then found out about as many names as different zip codes or phone numbers at the end, then I would say: No, my hypothesis was wrong, it is not. But if I find many names & the same zip code or similar phone numbers, then it means that they actually live together in a certain area. the data was there, but I had to find that information out first. Someone had to come up with a hypothesis to test & interpret that..

So where does meaning come from anyway & how is information generated?It's clear that there are many different opinions about what information is & where & how it's created.

Naturally, I think of Claude Shannon & Warren Weaver in particular & what they have to say about information.

I know they were both very sad that their field was just called information theory because they claim - & I agree - that what information theory is about is not information.

The same person goes back into the hall & asks again, "Is anyone here?"

It is therefore the situation that determines in this case how the respective statement is to be interpreted or can be interpreted.

It is often said that anyone can now have access to this information highway & superhighways. We should put a big question mark behind this statement. I'll come back to that, but before I do that, I want to explain a little more about what is meant by networks & the World Wide Web. It's easy to understand in a sense. There's data stored in devices. For example, this could be a computer itself with data stored on the hard drive, or it could be a disc, or a tape, or whatever. The computer can get at this data & pass it on

to be connected to a network, in the sense in which phones are connected to each other. You could try calling me on the phone in Cambridge, Massachusetts if you have the right number. The trick to doing this is simple: my phone number is unique, it is *unique*. No one else has this phone number. First comes the area code, here from Germany 001, that's USA. Then comes 617, that's part of Massachusetts, the part that I live in. Then if you call my office at the university, comes 253, that's the university, then 6033, & you've got my phone set stand in a house. It's similar with the World Wide Web. Instead of telephone numbers, we're talking about a so-called URL. That means *Universal Resource Locator.* The trick with the World Wide Web is that everyEach one gets an address.

The address has something to do with where the computer is located, just like with the phone.

It is unique, just like any other address.y unmistakable address on the net. It is *unique,* just like any other address. If you send mail there, it arrives at MIT first & is immediately forwarded to your current location. You can see how well this is working – so far at least, because I don't know how long it will go on like this – because when I'm sitting at home & I send myself a message via e-mail, i.e. to Sadie @mit .edu, sends a message to my display immediately after the last button press:

"You have new mail." It all happens incredibly quickly. If you follow this closely, you can see that different stations are passed through - via the Atlantic to the USA, from MIT back via the Pacific or via another route, it doesn't matter at all: the satellites are so high, they don't bother with such things. The message comes to me because it is clearly about the UR life for me

is "addressed," & it's happening in near real-time.

Anyone can have an »address« or a special page on the World Wide Web in this way that is uniquely defined & findable. This leads to the statement that today we are dealing with a completely new democratic medium. Similarly, long after Gutenberg, it was claimed that the newspaper was such a new medium for democracy. One of the things you need to do is have a little money. Nowadays, with the new technical possibilities, anyone can actually write an essay, for example, & then enter their messages into the network. So can many others who have access to it, whether they live in India or in Japan or in Berlin. Once that is there, then practically everyone who has access to the World

Wide Web at all also has access to this communication. Possibly this is a new starting point for a better understanding towards a worldwide democracy & this leads us to the concept of the "global village". The old idea is suddenly revived: if I actually publish a small newspaper, everyone in our "small village" will notice & read it. It seems to be the same with the web. Anyone can write whatever they want, & anyone can read it, at least in theory.

As I have already mentioned, such a network was first developed at various American universities around 1963 on behalf of the US Department of Defense. I was then able to communicate with my colleagues at Stanford over these networks just as easily as with anyone else connected. Later, the circle that was involved increased more & more, & the performance possibilities were significantly expanded. The speed at which data was transmitted at that time was about 300 bauds. Today the standards are 14,400 bauds & more. At the time we didn't know how slow it was at 300 bauds, but at least it had become technically possible to communicate using a new method. Around 1963, these were the first e-mails in human history, so to speak.

The year 1963 was significant in other ways. It was the year President Kennedy was shot & it was the year the war in Vietnam escalated. You all know the events around 1968. There was considerable resistance to this war, especially at the universities & supported by the students . All kinds of demonstrations & *teach-ins were* organized there, & this often happened simultaneously in many universitie sAn ted network existed. I want to emphasize this again: It was a network that had been developed in the interests of the military & was also financed by them alone. Nobody paid for it, only the Pentagon! The amazing thing was that we never heard "a peep" from these people. They never said: "You really can't do that" or "We don't like that." We were absolutely free in using & dealing with this network. & this is how it should be in principle with the World Wide Web today, although there are limits due to human custom & decency that must be observed.

Some of the crucial questions at the moment are: who has access to this matter & who belongs to the information society? How to identify members of the information society? Today, as a member of the information society, you certainly have access to the World Wide Web, but I can't say for sure who belongs to it. But it seems clear to me that members of the information society certainly have credit cards in their pockets or have a bank account. & now we can ask ourselves how many that actually are. I don't know exactly what it's like here in Germany, but I do know that most people on this planet don't have a credit card in their pocket or access to the World Wide Web. Even in a country as rich as the United States, a great many people still have no access to it. That's maybe a third of our population in the United States, & it's likely that these people will never have access until a lot of things change radically. Well, I think that if we are now talking about *global village* , then everyone should really be involved in a certain way

in a certain sense, even on purpose, because it's very convenient to think like this: "Well, everyone has access to it, everything is very democratic & all that." But in reality it's just not like that!

The word village *also* evokes the association & the idea that the world has become smaller in a certain sense. I think everyone will agree. We experienced a kind of implosion; I say implosion instead of explosion because explosion means things fall apart. Implosion means things come together. I can still remember very well that until recently it wasn't that easy to call Tokyo from, say, Berlin or Boston. It wasn't that long ago that you had to register the conversation. The operator, as the women on the switchboard were called at the time, would have said it could take three hours or two days. They would tell you they would call you back if they could connect. & after three hours, or after two days, or whatever period of time, you finally got a call & were told that you would be connected in a few minutes. Then, in principle, one could speak to find out the price of a certain stock in Tokyo, for example. But one must also realize that a large part of the time on the phone was spent frequently asking the question: "Can you hear me?"

Fortunately for us today this is usually a thing of the past.

I am very impressed how quickly the development has progressed since then. We can read & take cognizance of the overall status of all stock exchanges on this earth in practically real time

become more manageable. Something else has also changed with it. Many of the transactions that take place there on a daily basis no longer represent an actual investment in an industry or anything, but rather are cards thrown on the table in the hope that they will be worth much more in a short period of time. I would say that what we have today is one, one-off, gigantic casino. We have to realize that the governments & banks of the big nations together have less money today than the internationally operating circles of speculators. This raises serious questions about what this means for politicians & their opportunities to exert influence, as well as for economic stability worldwide. Under these circumstances, who governs? Whoever can influence the value of the dollar – & the circles of speculators can do this better than ever before – can also exercise a certain amount of power. These people, who can do this, have not been elected by anyone, nor are they democratically controlled by anyone. If we think about it, then we see that the world today doesn't look like a big village at all.

Unless we just mean that "information" - better said, "signals" - can fly around the world at lightning speed thanks to new technologies .

In principle, one could say that everyone should have access.

There is already a somewhat older model for this, which we know in the form of television.

Television, when it was first introduced, was hailed as something that will unify the world & have a democratizing influencenoblest & finest inventions that the human genius has produced. This also applies in the same way to the World Wide Web, the networking of the world. I believe that everything that has been made possible by satellite television & data transmission, human ingenuity, engineering, science & especially the natural sciences can be understood as a masterpiece of mankind. This is a real achievement, an *achievement,* all of these together. One can be proud of being a human being when one considers who & what all had to work together. I'm thinking of mathematics, physics, to name just a few disciplines, which have contributed to the fact that there are stationary satellites up there in the sky today, which always remain above a point on earth & in this way enable modern data transmission. Well, calculating how they get there & how they stay there is quite a feat . It also took the chemists & the meteorologists to develop the rocket technology to today's standards. Knowledge of navigation & communication technology is just as important. One must be clear about this: Signals, for example, are broadcast from a television transmitter & bundled onto a very small area & sent up to the satellite. They are received there & remain coherent on their way, ie the bits do not mix. We could be receiving those signals right now, right here in this room. All we need is the right device & we would receive an image or several programs, even in color & in real time. That this is technically possible is really amazing. & the same applies to the example of electronic mail via email, which I mentioned earlier when I send myself a message that goes around the world & gets back to me almost immediately. This doesn't just happen sporadically, but thousands of times at the same time. It's also absolutely amazing to me how this became possible & works thanks to the many inventions & engineering deeds. As I said, you can be proud when you think about it. It should be remembered that less than 40 years have passed since the Soviets first succeeded in launching a satellite into space. I was just in Europe at that point in 1957 & I still remember it very clearly. When I read that in the newspaper, one of my first thoughts was that Mr. Newton must be jumping in his grave for joy at this news & at the evidence that such a thing is possible. He already had the mathematical knowledge that indicated this possibility in the 17th century, but it had not been technically realized until the 20th century. It didn't take long for me to understand that for many people this fact was no reason to be happy. The Americans saw it as a hostile signal & as a threat. As you all know, this led to a tremendous effort by the USA to catch up with the technological advantage that the Soviets had at the time, & I certainly owe my own career to that fact in the end. The "Sputnik shock" led to a financial boost for the universities, so that many things were ręsęarchęd & pęoplę likę mę węrę now also ablę to tęach at a univęrsity from 1963 onwards.

Having outlinęd & acknowlędgęd thę scięntific & tęchnical achięvęmęnts that madę tęlęvision, thę World Widę Węb, & satęllitę communications possiblę, it is impęrativę that I addręss anothęr point that has bęęn nęglęctęd look at the content that is »transported« in the majority of these communication channels today! Imagine if there were still living beings somewhere up there who could receive our television pictures. What would they think of us? Do we humans have a reason to be proud of these achievements & what we are doing with them? I am addressing the nonsense that we broadcast 24 hours a day on the television channels & I am afraid that the same can be said about the Internet & a lot of the content on that network.

So, once again, this progress has two sides. It is really true, at present we have the ability to store & make accessible almost all contemporary human knowledge, & that is only a small part of knowledge from all times & epochs. Almost every question & problem today can be found somewhere on the Internet, on the World Wide Web. This is an absolutely imposing building. I can imagine a family visiting this attraction & maybe the mother will explain to the children that almost all the knowledge that is written down about humanity around us can be found here. & maybe the little daughter then says & thinks: "Well, let's ask a question & maybe we'll get an answer." In view of the abundance of data & materials that can be accessed on the Internet, it seems that we too now havę thę illusion that wę only nęęd to ask onę quęstion & thę right thing will comę out. Unfortunatęly, that's not truę for a varięty of ręasons. It doęsn't work likę a vęnding machinę whęrę I insęrt a coin & thęn what I want comęs out.

I would likę to add a little story from my

Family circlę tęll: My littlę daughtęr, shę was maybę 7 yęars old, sat with mę in thę car & thęrę was a camęra lying around.

Shę askęd mę: »What is thę connęction bętwęęn thę numbęrs 1,4;2;2,8;3.5;5,6 ętc.?«

so had ręad thę numbęrs on thę camęra lęns & wantęd to know why thęy arę thęrę thę way thęy arę thęrę.

I said, "That's a good quęstion."

I wantęd to ęxplain it to hęr, but first I was impręssęd & said, "That's a good quęstion."

& thęn shę askęd hęr:

"What's a good quęstion?"

& so I said to hęr: "That's a good quęstion, too."

I'm making distinctions with that.

To mę, a good quęstion is likę dęsigning an ęxpęrimęnt, ę.g. B. in physics.

First you havę to know a lot, & thęn you ęstablish a connęction & construct an ęxpęrimęnt in physics, for ęxamplę.

In this way onę thęn quęstions naturę.

Bęhind this is thę idęa or dęsign of an ęxpęrimęnt.

Thęrę arę trivial & lęss trivial ęxpęrimęnts.

My littlę daughtęr must havę known that thęrę was somę connęction in this sęrięs.

That's an idęa that maybę not ęvęry sęvęnyear-old child has.

I'm sure you'll understand if I add anything else.

The same girl later asked me, "Daddy, what time is it?"

& then added:

But I don't want to know how a watch is made right now." So much for my daughter & her questions as a child.

Now, if I come back to the topic of content & you want to know what I think about the Internet or about television, then I hardly have to say anything more about television, because that is obvious. Most of it is triviality, nonsense, or nonsense. With the Internet, things are a bit different. I just made the analogy with the Congress Library to show that there are many ways to get information here

What I have in front of me right now, when I look at the Internet as a whole, is more of a heap of rubbish, a heap of junk, as you can see in Bombay, & that's not at all desirable. In Bombay, for example, people not only live on the edge of this rubbish heap, they actually live on top of this heap. Among them are many small children, mostly naked, & they rummage about all the time. Every once in a while they find something they can use. Once in a while they find something to eat, or they just eat it. It's possible that there might be a pearl in there somewhere. It seems to me that the internet is similar.

So the internet can be described as a garbage heap with pearls in it. This accusation is countered with the argument that the Internet is the first to offer the possibility of obtaining a large number & variety of information. In certain situations one should be very careful with the word information. The signals in the computer are not information. There is only one way to make information out of signals, & that is to interpret the signals. Interpretation requires the use of the human brain, & of course interpretation means work. Regarding the garbage on the Internet, it should be noted that the Internet is now a mass medium. It seems to be a law of nature that any mass media produces 90-95% junk. All we have to do is watch the radio or television. In the beginning there were all sorts of hopes & predictions connected with the mass media. For example, it was expected that they would improve people's education. The same hopes are now being raised with the Internet. But I think anyone who wanted to deny that most of the mass media produces crap would have a very hard time arguing that.Of course, there are also pearls on the Internet. However, in order to find them, the user needs a certain level of competence. You have to decide on a specialist area that you are already familiar with. You have to know enough to be able to formulate a good question. If I go to the internet with a question about grammar, I can find a gold mine or a sack of pearls. However, it would not be enough to simply type the term »grammar« into a search engine. I must have a more specific question, & then I may come up with something that leads me to something new, etc. It's not junk, of course, but the simple surfing, following one link after the other, the random surfing, that very quickly leads to the accumulation of Garbage. The various chat groups & newsgroups also make it very clear that there is a great deal of nonsense at play.

I remember a very old medium, the message in a bottle. A very democratic medium. Anyone can take a bottle, put a message in it, & throw it into the sea. The only question is who reads it. So, the possibility that anyone can write something on the Internet doesn't mean very much. Throwing it in at random is just as useless as fishing at random.

A good analogy to the introduction of the Internet is the introduction of Citizen Band Radio in America many years ago. This is the possibility of having a radio transmitter & receiver in the car, but it only has a range of about 20 km. Anyone could have this radio.

There were different channels in it, one for emergencies, one for the police & many free channels. You could sit in the car & if you got lost, just speak into it:

"Can someone help me, I'm in front of City Hall." & then someone responded & asked, "Yes, where are you going?"

& then he helped you further. Some people had a radio like that at home & sat all day listening to it & giving advice. For two or three years this device was a must have. Everyone had to have this CB radio, it was even installed in new cars. A specific question like "I'm in front of City Hall & how do I get from here to anywhere?" would be of great help. But again, just like the other mass media, the content was ninety percent just air. they still have it. Also when CB radio was introduced, a lot was said about new possibilities for democracy, & yet it has disappeared again.

The same things that were once said about the possibilities of CB radio are now being said about the Internet: everyone has access, it's brand new, it's a support for democracy, etc. The Internet certainly contributes to the fact that today no state can shield itself in such a way, install news blocks or isolate its own people in such a way that nothing gets out. However, if I imagine a Stalin state, it would still be possible for the secret service to terrorize the population so much that they would hardly use this instrument. The secret service in such a brutal regime will eavesdrop & find out who is getting what messages from where. This isn't as easy on the Internet as it is on a radio station, but it's not impossible. One should not underestimate the totalitarian state, its power & its capacity for terror.

It is always important in which social environment a mass medium, no matter which one, is built

Every instrument inherits & maintains its value from the society in which it is embedded. In a »free« society, the Internet could be an aid to democracy.

I would like to mention something else related to the overestimation of technology. The recent mass protest against the WTO conference in Seattle was claimed to have been impossible without the Internet. This claim is false. That the protest gathering was supported by the Internet is out of the question. If there is a tool, then it matters, but it is not absolutely necessary for the action at all. Even if the telephone & the Internet are employed & used for political demonstrations, it does not mean that they were the main thing that brought people together for political action. In this sense, technology is often overestimated today. In 1968, at the time of the heavy demonstrations at the Democratic Convention in Chicago, there was no internet, & yet it didn't take long for people to realize that the police here had gone haywire towards the demonstrators. In that sense, technology can be overrated. Technology is always a tool that may or may not make certain things easier.

Finally, the question arises as to who is responsible for the content of the Internet, for Nazi websites or child porn? Where are the people in charge? The subject is very serious. Here I have to repeat that every medium is always embedded in the respective society. In terms of responsibility, I am thinking of such terrible things as the *My Lay massacre* in the Vietnam War. The lieutenant in command was accused, but didn't feel guilty, shifting the responsibility up to Captain Medina, who was behind the lines .Responsibility lies with the lieutenant below.

We live in a society in which there is a great

reluctance to take on responsibility. This is a general social phenomenon. So we shouldn't be surprised if, in some context that we hadn't thought of before, we encounter exactly this phenomenon of denial of responsibility. Responsibility is not a technical issue, but a social one. Our social condition is characterized by a denial of responsibility. Our society has developed the technique of distributing responsibilities so that no one has them.

But maybe it is also a characteristic of our time that a large part of the communication in the networks can be regarded as nonsense. There just doesn't seem to be that much creativity among us humans. We have so many TV channels that broadcast programs 24 hours a day that it's certainly not possible to feed them all wisdom. So why should this suddenly be different on the Internet than on television?

Today we often speak of a knowledge explosion that we are confronted with. We *knew* this word before the internet came into fashion. We talked about it maybe ten or fifteen years ago, but it wasn't true then either. What we had & what we have is more of a »nonsense explosion«. It's just like that that most of the papers published in scientific journals today are hardly read by anyone anymore. There is a tremendous flood of publications, but few actual new discoveries. Just look at how many scientific journals there are today & compare that to the situation 10, 20, or 30 years ago. Thanks to PC technology, the proportion of texts & publications is increasing exponentiallyMIT, have shown us that you can even write papers that you don't even have to read yourself. All of this can be done with the help of the computer. In most cases, the mass of publications that are being released into the world & the data networks are not of the quality that I would wish for. Unfortunately this is the case. At the end of my remarks, I would like to give a stimulus for reflection & discussion, or even provoke a little by asking a question. My question is: who is subject to the power of technology? Is it the one who applauds them indiscriminately, or is it the one who takes a critical look at the situation &, under certain circumstances, can also say »no« to certain developments?

The human image in the light of artificial intelligence

Each era has its own mythologies. In earlier times, the mythological lore of modernity was systematic & had great permanence; mythologies survived for hundreds, even thousands, of years. Time seems to flow faster & faster. We observe this with a certain amount of anxiety, both in international world politics &, for example, in our schools. The mythologies of our time are just as fast-moving. They seem to come suddenly, to determine our worldview, & then just as suddenly to give way to our thinking in favor of a new mythology.

I'm thinking here, for example, of our once mechanistic world view, which was suddenly called into question by Albert Einstein & his theory of relativity. On the one hand, Einstein was hailed like a star, while on the other hand, paradoxically, the rumor was spread that only five people in the world understood relativity at all, which of course was wrong. An important idea was thus misunderstood & gave rise to a widespread misconception.

Today, science dominates as the foundation for almost all of our ideas of what the world is like, why the world is the way it is, & how & who we ourselves are

sustainably dominant world religion! There are novices, for example the students, there are priests & bishops, even cardinals: the Nobel Prize winners. Whether there is a pope or not is debatable. There are churches, even cathedrals.

The necessary rituals are not lacking either - there are sects, heresy, excommunication & much more. The surest sign that science has become a religion - one could also say »ideology« - is the scientific belief of most modern people. It hardly differs from the religious belief that is still to be found today. This, too, was based on the authority of their priesthood - just like the belief in science today. For example, modern man believes that the earth rotates around the sun & not vice versa. But the reality before him contradicts this thesis every day! People see the movement of the sun & the stillness of the earth with their own eyes.

Of course, the triumph of the princely daughter of natural science, modern technology, has a lot to do with the enormous amount of belief in natural science. The almost magical devices that science-based technology has introduced into our everyday lives are working. We can test Boris Becker's tennis skills in Frankfurt or

Tokyo

»real time« & *livingcolor in our living rooms. Our* hearts, kidneys, lungs etc. can be transplanted into other people & we fly fearlessly

across the continents & seas of the earth, just to mention three examples of the triumph of our technology.

The day-to-day demonstration of the power of our technology bestows almost limitless authority & credibility on the priests of the Church who make it all possible. But as the triumphs of technology accumulate, the underlying science becomes more & more abstract & thus more inscrutable, even more incomprehensible to the public, even to the educated public. More & more people are suffering to the point of desperation from the feeling of an irrevocable remoteness of a whole continent of fundamental knowledge of our time. This leads to a loss of self-confidence & self-assurance in one's intellectual abilities. The more the dependence on experts, including the priests of science, increases.

From a philosophical point of view, the most spectacular & therefore the most important magic device that technology has recently introduced into the everyday life of modern people is the computer. From the very beginning, the computer was described as a giant *brain* , characterized with human intellectual abilities, & generally presented as a »problem solver«. Heroic achievements were attributed to the computer. you lied Whether they knew that or not is still an open question.

They were certainly intrigued by the potential of the computer, & rightly so. But they weren't sufficiently aware of that

Difficulties of their self-imposed tasks prepared yetexperienced enough. Today, of course, this excuse is no longer sufficient. But the claims of the current generation of computer (computer) scientists are often as absurd, unfounded, rampant, & irresponsible as those of the first generation.

The public, already immobilized & demoralized about technology & science, now has to judge the claims of the computer world & sort them into categories like credibility & nonsense. She is just as unprepared for this task as believers were in the Middle Ages who wanted to evaluate the statements of their theologians.

The ideologue The biggest offenders are found among academic researchers in the computer science field that calls itself artificial intelligence or simply AI—especially in America.

KI - or AI (Artificial Intelligence) in the

English- speaking world - was founded in 1956 as a specialty of the general subject Computer Science (or "Computer Science").

From the very beginning, the AI split into two branches: the activists & the ideologues.

The characteristic of the activists is their interest in designing computer systems that do very clever & skillful work.

Works that would be recognized as the work of intelligent men were not known to have been accomplished by machines.

Activists love to learn how humans perform the tasks they want computers to do, & often use the insights they gain in their programs.

But they don't insist on calling their machines models of human behavior.

Their main goal is to design & build smart computer systems.s intend nothing less than to design models of human thought that lead people to

one should be far superior in the ability to think & on the other hand should provide scientific explanations of the thought process, the function of the human brain, the exact modus operandi of emotions, etc. Besides, the ideologues want their models to work in practice. The development of functional models is obviously less important than the claim that the underlying theories are at least plausible.

The activist branch of the AI has less prestige in the universities & in the public eye than the idealist branch. The main reason for this is that the activists are judged by their successful projects, not by what they might be able to accomplish next year

-often-distant—futures.

Some examples: The activists have created computer systems that play world-class chess. However, little has been learned about what goes on in the brain of a world champion at the moment when he decides his next move. But the computer scientists who later use such machines - that is, the power of such machines - to solve a great problem gain little prestige.

The ideologues speak & write very differently

ZeitschriftHans Moravec, Head of the Mobile Robot *Laboratory*

ofCarnegieMellonUniversity(Pittsburgh,PA)that each

"essential" human function, be it physical or mental, will very soon have an "artificial counterpart," & that robotics will create a machine that "thinks & acts like a human, however little it may resemble him in physical or mental details." It even goes so far as to prophesy that such machines

"prompt our civilizing evolution." Such

statements of the ideologists have different

Effects in the public: First, she with the deep pen

Second, to hint at what progress has already been made. & third, & this is particularly important, to propagate some concept of humanity as completely natural in society. This strategy is so effective because science has long shaped the human mind in this direction.

Few people today dispute that man is basically an information-processing machine, or that parts of living man can be replaced artificially or by donor organs. Almost all Western medicine is built on this materialistic hypothesis.

The belief that science has finally made it possible, on the one hand via AI & on the other via genetics, to produce artificial beings that not only function like humans, but are also closer to perfection than natural humans, has had a deep influence on the human image of our time. The critical questions that are always in the foreground are: What is the essence of being human? Which properties of human intelligence are *computable?*

Thecontroversyaboutwhichcharacteristicso fhumanintelligencemeasurementsimprecisel yintheformofcomputerprogramdegree to which a computer can learn to "understand" human language has occupied the artificial intelligence community for a long time . Now, because no two people have exactly the same life story, no two people can understand each other perfectly. But most of our understanding of language is in contexts that we share with other people. These shared contexts make it possible for us to understand what others are telling us. The mere idea of a linguistic message out of context & without any intention is an absurdity. The idea that a message can have meaning without there being a potential recipient to decipher it is just as absurd.

A crucial aspect of the life story of every human being is that each is born of a mother, has primitive biological needs that are satisfied by the mother or someone else in her place, has a human body that inevitably plays a role in understanding & knowing Feeling it is when he touches someone else's hand. The acquisition of this knowledge is certainly not exclusively a function of the cerebrum. The knowledge partly includes the sense of movement, its acquisition presupposes the possession of a hand, to name only the very minimum.«

An elementary example: what does it mean to feel a hand on your shoulder? The only way you can give me a serious answer to this is to tell a story: A young man had a fight

with his girlfriend, & she had himdeserted. &
now he's sitting in the library, trying to work,
very distracted, & suddenly he feels a hand
on his shoulder. Or another story: someone
is being interrogated by the police; he was
sitting on a bench in the station waiting room
& suddenly he felt a hand on his shoulder.

It becomes clear that both feelings can only
be explained in context, because the deeper
meaning is a completely different one. To
judge these one must have life experience &
human sensibility. In other words, there are
things that humans know only because they
have a body. No organism that does not have
a human body can know these things in the
same way as humans. Any symbolic
description of this knowledge must
necessarily lose information which, on the
other hand, is crucial for some human
purposes.

It seems to me that this is an elementary
point. For the *artificial intelligence* elite to
believe that feelings such as love, sorrow,
joy, sadness, & anything that stirs feelings &
emotions in the human psyche, can be easily
translated into a machine artifact with a
computer brain shows, I think, a contempt
for life, a denial of their own human
experience, to say the least. I wasn't at all
surprised when I heard the American
philosopher Dan Dennett say:

"We must rid ourselves of our reverence for life if we are to make any progress with artificial intelligence," & even less so when computer scientist Douglas Hofstadter declared that "all things considered, the human race is not the most important thing in the universe."

Ideas, even wrong ideas, have power. The idea that a human being is an object, separate from their environment, from their fellow human beings, or at least separable – for scientific purposes – is wrong & dangerous. You

comes about & gains influence only because of modern man's subservience to science.

Can the computer understand people & why do we need

at all people?

I would like to start with the second question. In discussions about the future of humans & computers, the sentence is often heard: »In principle, a computer can do everything.« Here the question arises: If the computer can really do everything, why do we need artists at all? Or even: Why do we need people at all? I have colleagues who have been helping to answer these questions for many years. & their answer is: Correct

,we don't need people. You say we should make getting rid of people our research goal. You'll tell me that you don't believe that, that you think that's an exaggeration. I encounter this reaction again & again, in Germany, abroad everywhere. & yet I have to tell you, it's not an exaggeration. This attitude is exemplified in the book *Mind Children by Hans* Moravec, the scientist & director of the *Mobile Robot Laboratory* at Carnegie Mellon University in Pittsburgh, Pennsylvania. This book claims that in 40 years there will be robots with roughly the intelligence of humans. & it won't be long before the computers realize that they can get along much better without us humans. Then they start *wanting* to get rid of us. & that does n't take that long

humancultureandeverythingwehavebredisno tworthverything.Oryoucouldsay:Theserobots willkeepeverythingandcarryon.Wecanrelyont hem.Inthiscaseitmeansthesecond.

In *MindChildren* it is claimed that the computer could capture the whole human being. Not just in principle or in the abstract, but specifically for a very specific person. I can be captured into a computer. & when that has happened, then that computer is me. Not a copy, not a simulation, not a depiction, erich. Even in this low-brow intellectual circle, I can probably assume that everyone knows the American television *series* Star Trek. From there they have to be brought back into the spaceship. To do this, they speak into the microphone of their transmitter: "Beam me up, Scotty!" Scotty is the man who operates the instrument that will help them get back. & then they suddenly reappear in the spaceship. How is this done in this *Star Trek story* ? The person who is to be "beamed off" outside of the spaceship is broken down into its smallest parts by a set of instruments, analyzed so to speak. & this analysis is then beamed to the spaceship, where it is reassembled. Then it is back. But this is actually not the same person, it is not the same atomic molecules, it is a restoration. I mention this because Hans Moravec himself cites this example as an analogy for what will be possible in the near future.

HansMoravechatseenthatwhenheproposes thethesisthathumanscannecompletelybecom econceivedbythecomputer,thequestionmust be:Whatisessentialtobeinghuman?Andto his credit

he even put the question in the right place in this book. His answer is — I'll shorten that a bit:

Man is a lot of information. & what to do with the body? He answers that too. I'll say this in English first:

"The body is only jelly." It's nothing but the jelly that holds the whole thing together. For example, if we have Beethoven's 9th symphony on a CD, then we have the huge long string of numbers that contain the information »9. Symphonie« is recorded on the medium CD. & the body has roughly the same function of being the storage medium for a certain amount of information.

MindChildren & about *Hans* Moravec. There are three universities in America that are leaders in the field of artificial intelligence. They are Stanford University in California, Carnegie Mellon University in Pittsburgh, Pennsylvania, & MIT in Cambridge, Massachusetts, where I am. It is noteworthy that this Hans Moravec is the director of *the Mobile Robot* Laboratory at this leading university, not at just any university. Perhaps more importantly, the book was published by *Harvard University Press* . That means it's been read by a lot of people in Harvard who think it's serious science, not *science* fiction. The book is taken very seriously. What can one say?

The book claims that humans are underdeveloped & that today we know better & can do better. Then the question arises: Better than what? Better than what? & the answer is: Better than women can when they give birth to life. We see that these poor beings that are being born are weak, that we can make them useful very slowly, but it takes a long time & it is very

problematic. So these are mistakes. We can do better today. We can make artificial life that is far better than humans, far more intelligent than humans, & that is immortal. That's a big theme in this book, that robots are immortal. Why immortal? Precisely because the essence of man is information. & information can be copied with absolute accuracy in digital form, like a compact disc. For example, Hans Moravec says that if he sees that he will be run over by a car & killed in the next minute, then he can very quickly - the word is *downloading* - very quickly transfer himself into a computer, i.e. hand over his information, & then he lives on. & he doesn't just live further, he is also immortal. That is, if this computer rusts a bit, if it no longer works well enough, then this knowledge, this information, can be passed on to another computer. In this sense, human culture would then be saved & will be further developed.

In my opinion, man is not just information, & therefore I consider the reduction of man to a storage disk to be impossible.

There are a number of sub-questions to the question "Can the computer understand?" Does understanding have anything to do with art? Withcreativity? With production of knowledge? Can the computer produce at all? A side question that might already be an answer: Can a nuclear power plant produce energy?

Is understanding a necessary condition for creativity? & here I would like to quote something - also not exactly my favorite book - Sherry Turkle, *The Desire Machine.* In it she tells of a child. It's about the computer doing something unexpected. Sometimes it reacts one way, sometimes the other. That's what the children who play with it say: the computer

cheating us. To this another child replies: In order to cheat, the computer must know that it is cheating. From this I make: In order to be creative, the creative instrument, e.g. the human being or the computer, must know that it is creative. I don't know if I can defend this to the end or not, at least that seems plausible to me. Are we in the process of making a new human? & when I say "a new man," I think of the hopes awakened in the Russian Revolution. The hope was that communism would produce a new man, of course a better man.

Now I want to come back to the question: Can the computer understand? If the answer were no - & by & large I think it is no - then many papers on this subject are hopeless, or at least so limited that the great euphoria with which they are often presented is misplaced. Can the computer understand? One could also ask: Can humans understand? & then I would ask further: Can people understand absolutely? Can a single person seem to understand others completely? Here too the answer is: No, we cannot. I want to give a few examples. There was once a quartet in the music world, we will never see the same again. It was Rubinstein, Piatigorsky, Haifez, & Primrose—the older folks among us may remember the Four Heroes of Musicians—& they played New York's Carnegie Hall. & the Rubinstein had, as so often happened to him, lost the thread. Then Teer whispered to Piatigorsky:

"Where are we?" & Piatigorsky replied, "At Carnegie Hall in New York."

Another example that most of you will not understand, although they are very simple words & I am describing a very simple experience that I actually had . However, most of you will not understand it .

Some yes, but not all. I was in New York, in Manhattan. On the street at 3:00 p.m., a lot of people, a lot of cars. I'm standing at a traffic light, waiting for the light to turn green so I can cross.

"Are you a Jew?" I answer: "Yes." Then he goes on to ask: "What time is it?" Over.

That's the whole story. How should we understand this? I would say most of you don't get it. You might laugh if it were explained, but it can't be explained. You just have to have a life story that makes it possible to understand that.

I'm talking about understanding natural language here, & I think that's the measure of how far we can go. For example, the computer can understand if I say, "I want that there." We have seen that there are devices that can respond in this way, but this is only possible in an extremely limited context. Now comes the question: "Is machine translation of natural languages fully possible?" & the answer is simply: "No, it is not possible." One can also omit the word "machine". So, is translation from one language into another fully possible? & the answer is again:

'No.' A Japanese man who had translated one of my books once said to me: 'It's very easy for you authors. You write whatever occurs to you. But Ihal's translator must try to understand it.' & it is true that one cannot translate without first understanding. That was the big mistake when, about 25 years ago, people at Harvard University were working hard to translate English into Russian & vice versa. The computer should do this work. They thought he'd take an

English dictionary & a Russian dictionary & translate

get the syntax right. Of course that didn't work. The basic requirement, understanding, was missing.

Why can the computer understand so little? Because the computer has no semantic relation to things in the world. In the computer everything is abstract, the bits or the electrons are racing around & what they mean the computer cannot know, it does not care. That's saying too much, "he doesn't care." He can't "take care" at all.

I have a little story about it. Suppose a powerful little computer, a personal computer, maybe solar or battery powered, is being transported from somewhere in Nevada to somewhere else in Arizona. On the way, it falls off a truck. It's lying there in the middle of the desert. They want to know: what kind of thing is that anyway? & they start measuring, & they're very, very careful not to destroy anything & even - although that's not quite possible - not to disturb what's going on inside the pc. After a period of time, they know the state of the computer, I mean that technically, "the state of the computer" at a given nanosecond. & since they're very smart, they've also grasped the state-changing rules, so now they know everything there is to know about the computer. Now you can predict exactly what this computer will calculate in the next million years. (That's not entirely true either, but it's good enough for this purpose.) Now you know everything about the computer. You know what the state of the computer will be in the next nanosecond & what the state of the computer will be in ten minutes. Now the question arises: do you know what the computer is doing?now tell you that the computer is calculating a weather forecast. Could the beings--or could a human--figure that out? Although they now know everything there is to know about computers, they basically couldn't.

I would also like to say something about the problems that are being worked on in science. It is perfectly clear that we could ask an infinite number of questions about nature, but in fact, since we die, we only have finite time. Therefore, we must carefully select the questions that we ask nature. There is a choice, & it is associated with values. No, they chose them. I know all these people, & I have to say that they are nice people in the usual sense: they have children, & they are as good to their children as any other human being. Sometimes good, sometimes not so good. They are not devil characters or anything. But how do they come to be dealing with these issues & driving their research in this particular direction? I have to say I can't answer that question, & I hope that university students will set themselves the task of analyzing who these people are & what they mean.

One thing is clear: there are men. There are no women. & not because there are not enough women in computers

– there are a lot of women in computing. Or because there aren't enough women in computer science at American universities. That's not true either. We have two or three female computer science professors at MIT. It's also not true that women don't work in AI at all, but they work very differently, not in that direction, & that's remarkable. I would like to say that I have been involved with compulsive programming for a very long time

have dealt with. There are compulsive programmers all over the world, everywhere. In the Soviet Union, in China, in South America, in the USA, in Canada, everywhere. Here in Europe too. & the funny thing is that they're all men. There are no women who are compulsive programmers. There is none. I've been looking for a long time in the last 20 years, all over the world. Sometimes someone says to me: "Oh yes, there are." If I then ask: "Yes, who is?" the answer is usually:

"Well, I don't know her, but a friend said he

knew someone, etc." But you can't find her. There must be a reason. Is there a connection between compulsive programming & this drive to become God? I don't know, although I've been told more than ever that I believe there is such a connection.

If we look more closely at the people working in this direction, we discover a contempt for biological life, & later we will see that it is a contempt for life in general. It was a long, long time ago that Minsky, one of the founders of the whole subject, said: "The brain is merely a meat machine." That cannot be translated exactly into German. An attempt might be: "The brain is just a meat machine." But something is missing from this translation. In English, there are two words for flesh: *flesh* & *meat*. "Flesh" is living flesh. But "meat" is dead flesh that can be fried, that can be eaten, that can be thrown away. To say so explicitly: »The brain is ...«, & then the word »merely«, nothing other than »ameatmachine«, shows the tendency to despise life even in the early days of artificial intelligence. This goes so far that man is viewed as a misdevelopment of nature or of God, who, as I said, is a mediocre

engineer.

The key words God as architect, God as engineer often appear in the discussion. My colleague Minsky also uses such terminology, but what he says is: Unfortunately, God was just a mediocre engineer, & now we can do it much better. & then, when it finally succeeds in a few cases - mostly it doesn't work at all - a really "good" person with high intelligence, of course, so to speak

"manufacture," then he dies & all is lost. This is a misdevelopment of evolution, or perhaps a mistake by the architect & engineer God. We can do it much *better* today human race is not the most important thing in the universe. This is reflected in the book *MindChildren.* If you now look a little more closely at this sentence, "The human race is not the most important thing in the universe," then you have to rule out that something else is more important. If you now think away the unimportant, i.e. the human race, then you could ask: Yes, to whom is the other more important? In America today we have one of the perhaps most important philosophers, Daniel Dennettander Tufts University, who says:

»We have to get rid of our reverence for life in order to be able to make further advances in artificial intelligence.« Not just anyone, a recognized professor represents & teaches such a thesis

his university, & I was the only one, I think, who voiced a word of protest. Nobody else protested. Maybe it has something to do with America.

Something else about the robots. I said machines cannot understand because they have no actual connection with the world, no semantic connection with things in the world. But that could be corrected by making robots that can move & that have all the tools we've seen here. Robots that can sense, touch, see, hear, etc. & if you let them loose on the world, like four or If you get five together in a room, then they start to have a story. & that story & that experiment & that change isn't programmed then. The possibilities are programmed, but not the change itself

"Experiences" that such a robot can have are not programmed. Then these robots have semantic connections to things in the world, in their world. Then they have a story, their story.

Is it still possible to deny that the computer can understand? The argument would be quite simple. Because now the computer has a story too. We are all the result of our history. All beings are the result of their history - not only that, but also that. But we cannot absolutely understand each other because we all have a different history. Every human being is a special case, every human story is a special case. But we can understand us because we have to share a certain part of our history. I'm also talking now about the Aborigines in Australia or about people who lived 3000 years ago. Anyway, they were all born of one mother, anyway, they all had the task of separating from their mother, & I mean not just physically, but mentally. Not an easy one

Task. & they all also have biological needs that are the same for all people. This is how our common story begins. When we are socialized, we are socialized as Germans, as Americans, etc. & then we start to be different. But we mostly live in one world. This can be in Cambridge, Massachusetts, or in Hamburg. We always have experiences that connect us. But not absolutely. The stories of Westerners, whether American or German, are much more alike than those of an American & those of a Japanese. Their socialization just went differently. There are areas where we cannot communicate. That doesn't mean that the Japanese can't tell me what's difficult for them or tell me something about their life or that of their children. It's also not that I don't understand enough to be able to answer properly. I can. But I can

eg not deciding whether it would be right for his daughter to go to university or not. Or whether this university or another would be recommended. I can't because I'm not socialized as Japanese. I really don't understand his problems. I listen, I can understand - in terms of language understanding on a certain level - but I shouldn't intervene. & I think that's the same with the computer has life experience.

In conclusion, I think it is important to say that death plays an important role in the development of human culture. Death is necessary - not just a mistake made by God

Culture handed over again & again to the new generation. My colleagues see here the difficulties associated with the transfer of a huge amount of information. & they feel that an exact copy of the *infoset is the best* solution. However, I believe that the next generation has the task of absorbing & restoring the knowledge & experiences that have been passed down: *to recreate.* It can't do that through bit -by-bit acquisition. & because this next generation has a different life story than their *parents* , the restoration will be more than just a copy of the knowledge & experiences inherited.

The computer & the natural sciences

Norbert Wiener wrote a book a long time ago: God & Golem Inc., also known as »Gottund Golem GmbH« . *Norbert Wiener, who has since died, is a former colleague who is, as one might say, the inventor of cybernetics.* He introduced the word cybernetics into the language, so to speak, & very early on saw a connection between technology & evil in the world. He also recognized the computer as an instrument that will probably dominate us at some point. Norbert Wiener published - I think it was 1946 or 1947 - a letter he sent to a colleague who had asked him to send him one of his works. In this letter he clearly says that he no longer does that. He does his work, but he won't pass it on because he knows full well that his work in cybernetics & mathematics will be used with the ultimate purpose of making rockets that can be shot from one continent to another. That was in 1946 or 1947. I tell this story simply to show how early Norbert Wiener saw the connection between science & the military. Norbert Wiener, who studied at Harvard, began teaching at MIT as a very young man & naturally knew that MIT was already very closely connected with the American military.

God & Golem Inc. - it's been a long time since this book came out. Now I want to say something about that. First of all, myths like the golem myth keep popping up, they're ancient. For example, they show up in the Greek tradition, in the ancient Greek literature, I think completely

especially to Pygmalion. He made the statue of a very beautiful woman & then finally breathed breath into her so that she came to life. Then he fell in love with this woman, as the story goes. We also know other examples like that, the golem is one of them, including Frankenstein, & today, I think, when you talk about things like that, you think of the robot. We humans imagine something like that today, & maybe that's our golem. I also think of the computer that just sits on a table like the PC & doesn't move at all, but still we sometimes see it as a golem. Just think of the so-called expert systems. I have experienced that the *Mephisto* computer that plays chess is also considered a dangerous instrument in a certain sense. I don't see it that way, I have to say, but that's a completely different matter. Perhaps I should also say that the game of chess is in the area

»Artificial intelligence«, as this area is now called, plays a very special role. It has long been known that the game of chess involves intellectual abilities. Now, if we can get a computer to make the next move in chess, that is, actually "play" chess & eventually maybe even win, then we have to mimic a lot of psychological problems & maybe different brain functions so that would be a good measure of how far we've come. However, it turns out that is not the case at all - this is not a criticism of artificial intelligence. It simply means that computers have become so much *faster & so* much larger in their functions & in their storage capacity that the chess games that computers like *Mephisto* do today are simply due to this raw power & has very little to do with what goes on in our brains when we play chess ourselves.

The legends & myths I just spoke about

I would like to add the example of King *Kong. Characters like King Kong or Tarzan - they are American phenomena, but also known here -* embody *notions* that ascribe *magical* powers to "primitive people", demi-humans or ape-men, so to speak. I think it is generally present in consciousness, or at least it is a fairy tale or a superstition, that such "primitive people" have special sexual powers to have. This is then transferred — at least in America — to the colored people. Another attribution of this kind comes to mind: Sadie Goebbels spoke of the "exaggerated intellectuality of the Jews" when the book burning took place.

In between there are connections - some connections that are very, very old & some that are much newer & more modern, but I want to single out the very old ones now that seem to have something to do with the evolution of our culture, maybe our humanity at all. It is just the case that many of the prophetic dreams that mankind has had for so long & that were perceived & canceled most particularly in the Greek myths have now been fulfilled or that we are very close to fulfilling them.

For example, I believe in Prometheus, who stole fire from the gods & was severely punished for it. I see an analogy to the mystery of nuclear power. Now we know how to set the whole world on fire, now we have stolen the fire from the gods, so to speak.

Icarus was taught to fly, flew into space, & then got too close to the sun. His wings fell off & then he fell & died. Today we have *spaceflight,* we fly around in space, more or less successfully, so we have also fulfilled this dream, & I think many others as well.

The bomb itself perhaps corresponds to the anger of the gods, from

that we read so often in the ancient myths. We are also in the process of trying - & we may succeed, & when I say "us" I just mean humanity - to create artificial life, & in two very different *ways* that we can put genes together to create an artificial being or modify ourselves in such a way that eventually humans would simply be unrecognizable today. The second way is at a different level, the engineer level. This brings me back to Daedalus, to his attempt to create artificial intelligence. This engineering attitude is quite explicit in the testimonies of Professor Minsky, Hans Moravec & other leading figures in this field.

According to this view, God was only a mediocre engineer & made many mistakes. Man as a whole is a misdevelopment, for example he gets sick & it takes so long to teach him intelligence at all, & when he finally gets old & maybe a little wise he has to die & all his wisdom is gone. That's not a good design according to this theory, & we'll just be able to do much better.

These are two variations of the golem dream: we try to either make gods or even become gods. At least we build things that we can then worship; I remember the Golden Calf here. It's almost - & I know it bothers some people when I say this - that science, modern science, claims to have seen the Promised Land. Here I am reminded of Isaac Newton's saying: "When I have seen far, it is because lightly on the shoulders of giants

Today science is on much higher shoulders, well, science sees the world from space & can see very far &, as I said, maybe promises that we're pretty close to the promised land.

It is often said that electronics in particular, if we act correctly in the next few years, can make our world a paradise, the promised land. I even believe that science has become the modern religion, so to speak. There are higher priests & cardinals, maybe even popes. There are great cathedrals, like the technical colleges of the world, especially my own, Massachusetts Institute of Technology. &, perhaps more importantly, modern science speaks, to a large extent, a secret language that the general public cannot understand, or at least think it cannot understand, certainly rightly so. I would say, here there is an analogy with the language of the ancient churches, Latin.

I remember my childhood when there was a magic spell in Germany that the older people here probably still know: »HokusPokusFidibus«. I think it was an imitation of what the priest says, sort of Latin, & of course it has magical powers.

We're doing about the same thing today, maybe I should say *you* 're doing about the same thing today, of course very modern. What I mean by this is that there are words that science adapts from common language for specific purposes. First of all, because of their original meaning. Then, however, they are somehow transformed & come back into everyday speech, but with a completely different meaning or even no meaning at all.

I'm thinking of a word that rushed this story not so long ago : disaster. It had a place &

its meaning in everyday language. Then there was & still is a *catastrophy theory in mathematics* - as they say in English, that is, catastrophe theory. With catastrophes, as we understand them in everyday language, well

eg a ship sinking, to do nothing at all. The theory of catastrophes is a technical matter involving complex mathematical systems. Suddenly the newspapers, the media picked it up & explained a lot of what was catastrophic. This is nonsense. The word "chaos" had a similar fate. It's spoken of in the same sense. Also, the ascribed meaning of left & right brain comes to mind now. Everything is taken up, catastrophe, chaos, & used completely wrong.

One of my young colleagues at the university made a very special computer & simulated the future of our solar system up to many billions of years. That can't be done with a very simple calculator, it just takes too long, but with this very special calculator, which can't do anything else, he calculated it & then decided that our planetary system is chaotic, but of course in this strictly mathematical sense. To put it simply, this has everything to do with the fact that very small changes at the beginning can have big effects in the end - again in a very mathematical sense. Then, a few days or weeks later, the newspaper says: MIT professor proves our solar system is chaotic. That is then understood quite differently. I really hope that the word "chaos" in this sense will disappear from everyday speech.

The two ways of artificially creating humans I was talking about come together in the claim that it will soon be possible to implant a very small computer in the brain on a single chip.

Now imaginę that this computęr has, for examplę, a foręign word lęxicon. If I am missing a word now, as it happęns to mę – I know it in Ęnglish, but I can't ręmęmbęr it in Gęrman – thęn I just havę to think about it, this built-in computęr starts up & thę word is thęrę, almost immędiatęly. Or solutions to diffęręntial ęquations, or just somęthing that can incręasę thę męmory capacity of our brain. That affęcts onę sidę.

Thę othęr sidę is now so far that wę havę - I'm missing a word in Gęrman, I'll say it in Ęnglish - wę havę *proposals* to takę parts from a livę animal & connęct thęm to a computęr. For ęxamplę, lęt's say - & this is a ręal ęxamplę - that all of a cat's vision machinęry, i.ę. thę ęyęs & thę correşponding part of thę brain, arę built into a computęr in ordęr to train thę computęr to sęę in this way.

In our mythology - I męan today's mythology that you sęę on tęlęvision, & I męan no harm by that - thęrę arę ręfęręncęs to this statę of ręsęarch. In thę tęlęvision sęrięs *ThęMillionDollarMan* , thę main charactęr is a human who probably had an accidęnt. Its lęgs & arms arę now ręplacęd with artificial lęgs, & it's madę up of lots of computęrs & machinę parts. You can sęę how gradually morę & morę machinę parts arę addęd. I think thęsę fantasięs arę vęry, very important: more & more machine parts, & finally you don't know anymore: is it a machine that has human parts or a person who has machine parts. That's where the two attempts to create artificial life come together a little. But I must say that we computer people have a greater hubris in this respect than do biologists. I have already mentioned the examples, Professor Minsky & Professor Moravec

Having time in this world in which DNA & the organs in general no longer play any role. Moravec supports the thesis that God was a mediocre engineer who made a great many mistakes, that man is a failure & that we can do it much better. So the question for me is: Who are we that can do it much better? It turns out that the people at the American university - I think also students, so not just the faculty, as far as I know, everyone who works on it - are men. There are no women. I can't help but think that what we have here is the flip side of the Oedipus myth. I think these men have a kind of womb envy, meaning they see that women can create life in this world, & maybe they think that's the only thing we men can't create. But we can! On this path that I have just described, & not only that, we can do much better. The creatures we make never get sick, never die, are instantly smart, don't need to be educated. I would like to emphasize that this observation should be understood in the context of golem, computer, man & woman.

My next observation has to do with eroticism. I don't know how many of you have seen the film *The Golem* that was shown in the town square a few nights ago. It's a famous film. There is one scene in it that I want to emphasize in particular: there is the golem, this big figure, a male figure, quite stiff, & at a certain moment there is a woman, the rabbi's daughter, he has taken her somewhere, she is passed out, he is bending over her, & he wants to kiss her. But it doesn't go that far. He doesn't get to it. I've forgotten what exactly is happening, but I can't get around to it. That emphasizes a certain eroticism that is always associated with these fantasies, with these fairy *tales &* myths famous film from the twenties. There's a scene in the movie where this big gorilla - I mean the size of a house or bigger - has in his hand a woman, a girl, & he's climbing the *Empire State Building with her.* She screams, & then she faints. This is a scene analogous to that in the Golem movie. We also find the same thing in the Frankenstein story, & then there's a movie that you may not know about, an American movie called *Westworld.* He plays in Arizona or Nevada, in any case in western America. There's a holiday camp where you can live medieval times or a movie western for two or three weeks. People fight & shoot each other & all that. Anyway, the people you meet in Westworld are cowboys. They are, of course armed, one is also armed. They bump someone in the bar, which is an insult, of course, & then you have to ask them to shoot. But the people you meet there are all robots. They look exactly like humans, you can't tell the difference at all, they look exactly the same, but they're robots & they're programmed so that the very human who's there for fun as a visitor wins the battles every time. In the world of the Middle Ages there are women who look exactly like human women. If there is a conflict later, you don't know whether this particular woman is human or robot. Of course, the reason for living in this world for two weeks is that you can do anything with these women. They're not real people at all, they just look like that, maybe they feel that way too, but, as I said, you can do anything with these women.

I think behind all these fantasies lies another fantasy that has to do with being allowed to do anything, especially sexually, with these beings who

They are not real people
– I already spoke about it – a racism.

Today's golem, as I see it, is not a doll, not a creature that looks like a human, it is almost always a man, a machine. To be able to say that, we have to expand the concept of machine a bit to include social orders & things like that. The fear of this machine, the uneasiness that plagues so many people, perhaps rightly so, stems from the fear or, should I say, the realization that the machine could or could get out of control, so that we are always recreating the phenomenon of the sorcerer's apprentice. So, first the machine does what we think it should do, but then it gets out of control. The bad thing about it – & this is where the nightmare begins in all these examples I have given – is that you can no longer switch off the machine. In the movie *The Golem* there is this - you could say almost modern - switch. Once the rabbi turns it off & the golem faints, but then the golem learned from it & now it protects that button, that switch. It's interesting that a very little girl - I don't know, four, five years old - sort of distracts him, & then she can turn him off.

But we are afraid that the machine will no longer be able to switch off. I would like to give a very serious example: The stock exchange system is such a machine that has to do with social order. Although computers play a role in this, it's not one computer that's broken, it's the whole system. I'm thinking of the October 1987 crash on the New York Stock Exchange. How did it happen? It's interesting: I was talking to someone about this recently & he said it must have been a computer glitch. I immediately said:

'No, everything worked brilliantly, there weren't any

Computer errors, in the end no errors at all, but nevertheless this catastrophe happened.« I think few people realize how close we came to a major catastrophe back then. I'm serious about how close we came then to the upheaval of the entire financial order around the world, across the globe. It was a very, very close thing. Yes, & how did that happen? First of all, there was a time when people started having personal computers, little computers on their desks, & various stockbrokers have bought such computers different people have written different programs, which I won't describe in detail now. Anyway, they're programs that analyze data & then send out an order to the stock exchange to buy or sell so many shares of this or that company for so much. That's pretty much how it was, & it's all calculated in such a way that if you do it real quick, you're guaranteed to make a profit. Well, you can't lose, it's all about seconds. One started by putting a programmed PC on his desk & made money that way. Then someone else did it, & then another, & then there were a lot of these computers, especially in New York. It is now worth emphasizing that these computers were not networked in the usual sense, meaning there was no cable or telephone line connecting all these computers, they were just stand alone computers. But there was a connection! The link was through the market itself. That means when a computer gives the order to buy, say, a hundred thousand shares of General Motors stock, the market senses it, & then the other broker computers sense it, & then they take action something. The whole is - & this is the important thing to understand - the whole, this whole set of computers, is a system. The parts are connected & form a system that can be analyzed with systems theory. & when you analyze that, you see that it is a system that is not stable in principle, which means it can tip over. A stable system can tip over a bit & then come back up, say a sailboat with a heavy centreboard. It tilts a little & then it comes back, it keeps coming back. But an unstable system like the one I'm talking about can just tip over, & that's what happened then. I can of course say much, much more on this matter, but I just want to emphasize that nobody designed this system. Nobody set out to make such a system, nobody made the system it also turns out that no one can turn it off. Stuff like this happens, & it's happening more & more often, it's happening today. The New York Stock Exchange suggested that all people shut down their systems if there was a risk that the system could collapse. If you recognize the appearance of a danger - of course also with the help of computers - everything should simply be switched off. But it turns out that there is no switch! You can say: "So please, dear broker, don't use that now," but then of course every broker has the idea that he's in a very good position if he's the only one using it now because the others are all doing what they're supposed to. So the system can't be shut down. & that's what I mean when I say that our golem isn't, not necessarily, a single machine or system in the usual sense. Here we are dealing with something that is really very reminiscent of the Sorcerer's Apprentice

Signs of our time that the responsibility here, one could also say the blame in this case, is not to be ascribed to anyone. You can't pick just anyone & say, "It's your fault. You did it wrong." As I said, it wasn't a computer error, everything worked as it should. & one could give many such examples.

The question that certainly arises here, at least the question that I'm going to ask here, is: are we helpless at the mercy of this golem that we made ourselves? I think the answer depends, among other things, on what we mean by "we" here. Who are "we" in this case? At this point I think of the sentence that we heard so often not so long ago, & I often believe with the greatest hope & joy: We are the people. I think the great men of the GDR - almost all of them were men - knew that the masses who kept shouting that were not drummed masses, as they were used to it themselves, but that each & every one of these masses recognized themselves as a member of the people, which should ultimately govern. All these many people were aware that that as individuals they no longer wanted to take part in lies, high treason & pure swindle. This golem, that is to say the rulers of the GDR at the time & everything that depends on it, was switched off & has become a heap of scrap & ash, like a golem in a film. Anyway, here's an example of how, if the "we" is interpreted correctly, we're not necessarily at the mercy of the golem, even the golem we made ourselves. But one must believe in oneself. Every individual must believe in oneself & in one's power, & that means one must not fail in the fantasy of powerlessness.

We are not powerless. We have experienced this everywhere, through many events that we have observed in recent years, through the victory of non-violent struggle almost everywhere in the world

– it has not succeeded in China, at least not yet. We are not powerless.

Now what does that mean for this golem we brought into the world? I mean especially us who live in the privileged First World, or what our President likes to call the "free world." What is the golem in our world? There are some, that's pretty sure, but I think the biggest is the madness that's going on in our world. I think every individual should decide to take a good look at it first & then decide to stop doing it. What I mean - it's just one example among many others - is the supply of arms to the Third World. I'm not specifically talking about the evil Germans who supplied so much to Saddam Hussein; I am well aware that in 1990 the United States supplied twice as many arms to the Third World as all other countries combined. It's just awful, it's obviously an export of poverty, because these countries in Africa & Asia can't afford the helicopters & all that. They have many other responsibilities. What do I mean, not going along with the madness? You could say yes, that means I should now write a letter, a letter to the editor, to various newspapers, maybe the *New York Times* or *Die Zeit* , protesting that we're still making arms shipments. Maybe you should do that too, but now that I'm talking about individuals, I think you should decide for yourself not to go along with this madness anymore. As said, there are many examples.

What do I advise e.g. B. Students at my university? That's pretty easy. It means becoming aware of what the ultimate goal of their work is, & I'm thinking here of research into making or improving the computer's vision

Work? Definitely one goal is to understand seeing better in general - that could perhaps also help the blind - in other words, simply to understand people better by understanding seeing better. That is definitely an end goal. But today - I'm not talking about tomorrow or the day after tomorrow or any other world - in our world today it is perfectly clear & absolutely guaranteed that any advances in this area will be immediately taken up by the military. The result is cruise missiles that can find their target even better. What I then advise the students, & indeed anyone listening to me, is to imagine that he or she is now sitting in that rocket, which is finding its way & which will eventually reach its destination. Then something happens, maybe an atomic bomb is thrown, in any case there is a big explosion, people are torn to pieces. I recommend then asking yourself if he's happy with that end goal, if he would push the button if he were there instead of here in the lab very far from this thing

We can ask:

About dealing with metaphors & our responsibility for the future

 Approximately how old is the theory or practice of teaching that you grew up with? It is often said that blackboards & chalk are outdated. It's a shame that with so much technological progress we still have someone up front with chalk & blackboard etc. Hubert Dreyfus, who is also here at this event, reminded me that the school system, when we've developed over the past 500 years or maybe even 2000 years, maybe today is optimal. It shouldn't be abolished. Anyway, I think we should be a lot more careful about how we progress. Now we regret that. We would have been better off if we hadn't pushed ahead with the dismantling so quickly.

Back to the school system. I'm not saying, especially in this context, that we should discount the possibilities that our new technologies offer us. That doesn't simply mean: more chalk or slightly larger blackboards. No, I'm not saying that. The new media are of course at the center of the new technologies that could be interesting for schools & that are important for children & for learning. They can perhaps be summed up by speaking from the screen, be it a computer or a television set. In any case, in America, children at home see every day that the screen is the source of truth

News, you watch the sport, etc. I say "truth," maybe I should say reality. You experience reality from the screen. & if we now use the computer & the computer says this & that on its screen, then one could assume that this must also be the truth or reality. That's a bit dangerous.

There is one more thing I would like to say very briefly about television, without going into how many hours adults & children in America spend in front of the television on average. I think the dangerous thing about television is that the knowledge, ie the data or what comes to us via the television, reaches us so absolutely effortlessly. We sit there & it's as if we're standing in the rain or as if the sun is shining on our heads - it's all happening without our doing! Herr von Glasersfeld remarked just yesterday: Knowledge must be built up by those who know with great effort, otherwise it will not last. I think it's the same with television, because the knowledge isn't built up. In this context I am thinking of the beautiful nature films & things of this nature that we see on television. We adults then say: how nice, our children know so much more, they've seen the whole world on television. But raising a little rabbit yourself, or growing plants, or watching a *Timelife movie about it on TV is a different matter* altogether.

With the help of the computer or on the computer you can create any world you want. Artificial worlds over which the programmer has all the power, which he can completely control. Today we can generally assume that the computer works as described in the instructions for use. However, it is not entirely certain that the *upgrading system also works* as it was written. The programmer knows that everything that happens there was made by him, including what doesn't happen, but what

should happen, so error. He is responsible for it. He can't go anywhere & say someone did something wrong here. This responsibility, the knowledge - it's my own fault, I have to be able to fix it, because I created this world & I'm the absolute ruler of this world - is of course fascinating the particles of an atom. That's beautiful, beautiful. We can even determine new laws of nature. I'm thinking, for example, of gravity & how it works. We all know the equations »Squared of the distance«, etc. We can replace them in the computer. It's not "Squared of the distance" anymore, it's something else, & it works. We have in this case made a world that is actually impossible in our world, & we can play in that world. This means tremendous power for the programmer - much, much more powerful & much greater than, say, Shakespeare had when he built his worlds for us. In practice this cannot be realized. If you want to see it at all, you either see it in your imagination - you can do that too - or you see it in a computer simulation.

In general, one could say that the computer can serve as a laboratory in chemistry, in physics, even in the behavioral sciences, & it is particularly important in economics.

A phenomenon from physics that I want to

mention, a very simple thing: there is a nail. There is a wire hanging from the nail, & on the wire is a key, & here are small weights. & now imagine students seeing this on a screen in a class. It's a very sophisticated simulation. A hand may appear, then take one of the weights & place it in the bowl. We then see that the wire lengthens a little. & then you add weight & weight, & the wire lengthens evenly by the same distance each time, up to a point. Then all of a sudden the wire stretches more than the last time, although the same weight was applied again. It's a phenomenon. The experiment was very clear & very nice to see on the screen. But there's a boy who says he doesn't get it. Asks:

"Could you repeat that?" & the teacher replies: "Yes, of course!"

A button is pressed & then the whole thing repeats itself. You can also interrupt the experiment & say, "You see, from here to here it's like this, & now it's different." But something is wrong with this idea. There are two things I would say that are wrong. First of all, such a simulation is a huge waste of energy & time. However, that doesn't bother me that much at the moment. What I mean is that maybe you can find a nail & a wire in every classroom & use it to do the experiment yourself. The experiment isn't something like the speed of light, or something we can't do at all. We could do this experiment by ourselves. Then the children would see how it works. That's one thing. The other - much more important, much more important - thing is the teacher's statement: »Yes, of course we can repeat that!« In nature, we can'tThere is very, very little in nature that is repeatable at all. Nature changes when we do something. When a student reports on an experiment he did in the chemistry lab & the numbers he gives as the result are identical to the numbers theoretically expected, then you know he didn't do the experiment. Only very rarely do the results of an experiment agree with those calculated in theory. This is a very, very important insight - I can't stress it enough. Especially the teachers should know this & talk about it with the students. This is just a very simple example of the greater cause

»Model«. What we do with computers are almost all simulations, models. You should know something about models. I wonder how many teachers around the world even know anything about model theories. To make that clear, I'll tell you a little fantasy story. Imagine a beautiful park. & in the park there is a beautiful mountain, a muddy mountain, because it just rained. On top of the muddy mountain is an elephant. & now a father comes with his little child. They're going for a walk. The girl sees the elephant, & since she knows very well that her father is a scientist, she asks him: "If the elephant starts to slide down, how long would it take for it to reach the bottom?" The father thinks about it & creates a model. In this model, the mountain is replaced by an inclined plane & the elephant by a mass point, plus a coefficient of friction that he certainly remembers. So he has a differential equation that solves & answers: "92 seconds, something like that." At that moment, the elephant starts to slide. The kid—remember, she's the daughter of a professor at a technical college—of course has a second stop watch

slide, she presses the button of the watch. The elephant slides down & let's say the clock reads 91.92.93 seconds, something like that. So another triumph for science. Now let's look at this model. What is included in this model & what is not included? Included in the model are - abstractly - the height of the mountain, the weight of the elephant, the coefficient of friction & a few other things. Really not much: four or five parameters, nothing more. Conversely, apart from these three or four parameters mentioned, every other fact, every fact of the universe is not included. It is not clear whether today is Tuesday, whether there is war in Yugoslavia, how much the sun weighs, etc. So almost everything from the whole world is excluded from this model. & it really is a triumph of science that the father was able to predict the outcome. I think that what Einstein meant when he said it's amazing, it's a wonder we can learn anything about the world at all using the weird methods of science. It's a very weird method, leaving almost everything out. & now I will claim that every model has this character. Many models mean many more parameters, but almost everything is always left out. & I think that's our world, our world of thought. It's almost entirely made up of models. Take the analogy or the metaphor, for example; we cannot think without these things. We cannot speak without analogies, models of metaphors, etc. This is a deep insight & learning this is something very meaningful. Once again I wonder how is this taught, how many teachers, now with or computers, know this & teach this?

In the behavioral sciences, e.g. B. *economics,* you put everything you can imagine into models. You have the whole world in a model, so to speak. & now it's started & we're relying on this model.

What I mean to say is that even if we combine our new technologies, *communication* & *computation,* so we can create powerful simulations, there will always be limits - whether the simulations are recognized as such or not is another matter. In every model there will be questions that we shouldn't ask the models. As nice as the rush that hits us with the new technologies is - if you can't talk about the limits, then it's not worth it, I would say.

What I have called models here is now commonly referred to as virtual worlds or virtual realities. This word is on everyone's lips now. About 20 or 30 years ago, a small, insignificant, especially scientifically insignificant branch started to produce *virtual reality : the computer world or computer industry. Virtual reality.* I'm sure you all know it. If you wear monitor glasses & see in three dimensions. You see a model & you're wearing a glove that corresponds to a hand that's actually in the picture. If you move your hand, that hand moves. As I said, this thing started 20 or 30 years ago. Great progress was not made in this time, only the computers have simply become very, very much faster. One may now extrapolate that a completely new method of seeing the world has emerged. Our children would live in such worlds. & there would no longer be any need to visit someone, because two people could plug into the same virtual reality & then they would have exactly the sensational experience, as if they had met. It is interesting, psychoanalytically interesting, that in such conversations - at least in the ones that I observe & participated - the question always arises as to whether one could have sex with the others in this virtual world.Answer: noterm *virtual reality* is on everyone's lips, & there is hardly a journalist who does not ask me about it in a similar way as just mentioned.

I've also heard lectures about *virtual reality here at this congress* . What we once called a simulation, or a program, or the course of a program, is now referred to by this term. You can see how this term *virtual reality* poisons our language, how the words have been devalued. But what I'm really getting at, & I'd like to add to what I've already said, is that we're always talking about a model. & all the limitation that I mentioned in the case of the model, that comes into play now. If almost the entire reality of the world, if almost everything is left out, then the statements that a model makes are very limited.

I think that if we now start talking about the new language of learning & teaching, & we now say that the new language is the language of computer scientists, especially that of extreme computer scientists, then that is a great pity. & I would like to add something else. The ancient languages of learning & teaching—like the streetcars of Los Angeles—should not be thrown away.

They sęrvę us, & by that I męan thę book &
ręading   in   particular.

Computer & Schools

It is often said that computers are everywhere these days & that young people should know what they are confronted with in the world. That's why it's necessary for schools to teach something about computers. But there are other things that are all over the world that we don't feel like we need to take the time to teach about at school.

I am especially mindful now that I have grandchildren. I have contact with small children again. It's been quite a long time since I've watched my own children - my youngest daughter is 28 years old. It's really amazing how quickly &, you could almost say, automatically, children learn the technology of this world without being taught it in school. Example: My three-year-old grandson & I get in an elevator & what he says? You all know what he says. He says: May I press the button? So, he understands button-pushing. This is a very complicated process, which, in a certain sense, means: When you press the button, something happens. It is also important which button you press. It means the elevator is going up & down now. His mother bought him a cassette player, but it's one made especially for little kids, made out of wood with big colored buttons. You can use it like a normal tape recorder. My grandson learned it straight away. It's also a fairly complicated instrument that we find almost everywhere in our world. Yet another example: I once saw a telephone on a pole outside in America, not a phone booth, & there is a little girl, maybe four or so five years old & she's holding the phone & speaking into it. How does she know what she's hearing is her mother's voice? & how does she know her mother can hear her when she speaks into it? This is a very, very complicated process, but the little kid got it, like most other little kids in our world. What I want to emphasize is that just because something is everywhere & we all use it, school doesn't necessarily have to change must take time to teach this.

Also, in connection with computers & school, a question that is often asked is what is the right age to give a child a computer or to allow him/her to have access to a computer? It is in a certain sense a question that is no longer necessary because the computer is everywhere.

For example, there is a computer in the clock that hangs in the kitchen, & in the washing machine, in the camera, in the car. Although not really necessary, there is a view that at some point it will be necessary to give a child access to a computer. I don't believe that because the people who believe it miss a few questions. One question, a very important question, is this: at what level of explanation do we want to explain the computer to the children? In English: "Atwhatlevelofexplanation?"Shall we explain to you how to operate a computer game, maybe an airplane simulator, which could be a lot of fun? Should we explain the computer to the children on this level? Then perhaps one can say something about computer languages, especially so-called higher computer languages. How does the computer work so that it understands this language?

Then there is what we call *machine language* – yes, & how does that work? You have to explain the switches of the electrical device, its architecture. It's not particularly difficult, I have to say, but you have to make a decision, you have to say: "We want this level."

Having said that, one must also defend one's idea by reasoning that it is precisely this level of explanation that one should start & stop with. Why this level? If you say, "No, they should also learn how these switches & this architecture work," then it doesn't take long before we're in quantum mechanics—I mean that—we're in physics. We certainly don't want to explain that to the kids at an early age. They can wait until they're at university to do that.

That this question is not answered, that even this question is not asked at all, says something about the incompetence of the people making these decisions for mainstream school systems.

Once again to the statement: the computer is there, it is everywhere, you have to learn something about it. A good question would be: are there other things that are also everywhere that we may have thought we should teach about in school? It turns out that of course we must have a small number of specialists, but otherwise we need to know very little about them. It makes me think of a device that we use every day. Certainly there is a whole lot of this equipment here in the room. If this device stopped working, surely in a week the world would be in great chaos. There would be many casualties, people would starve, many things would collapse. & the device I'm talking about, as I said, is everywhere. Personally, I have three of them with me right now, & many of you also have this device on your body somewhere think. This is exactly what is happening to the computer now & will continue to happen. The number of computers in industrialized countries today is certainly greater than the population of these countries.

professionals that we need, i.e. programmers, designers & architects, computer architects, is becoming smaller & smaller compared to the number of people who are actually directly or indirectly touched by the computer every day lost is simply not true.

But what is the gadget I'm talking about, the gadget almost everyone carries without realizing? The usual answers are pens - well, the world wouldn't starve if the pen stopped writing - or the watch - but I don't have three watches with me. I don't know what else will be advised. The device I'm thinking of is the electric motor. When I say I have three with me, it is because someone recently gave me this watch that contains three very tiny electric motors. Certainly many of you have a quartz watch that also has an electric motor inside. Of course there is also one in the fridge, in the camera, in the car. But we do not demand that every student first has to learn everything that has to do with the electric motor.

The school's resources are limited, not only in terms of money, but also in terms of time. The students are only in school for a very limited time. & if you now put something new into it, a new subject such as computer teaching, e.g. B., then something old must fall out. It's amazing how few people think about it. Something must fall out. What should it be? In America, it is customary to say: history. At the school or university where I teach – a technical university – I once heard in a discussion with students that you could do without history as a subject because what is being taught there (when something happened anywhere, keywords:

Columbus, America, 1492) is just that, whatthecomputercanretainsowell.

Something has to go, has to be replaced by the computer, & that tells us - & this is an important truth - that whether we want to introduce computers into schools is ultimately a matter of priorities. What is the most important thing? Of course, the question at least indirectly includes what the task of the school is.

Perhaps allow me to weep a little on your shoulder, in other words, to say something about the American school system, which is in a catastrophic state. What is happening & what you must not let happen here is that the issue I am about to speak about, the actual problems of the school are completely suppressed by introducing the computer as a solution. First of all, the problem is engineered; so technical questions are identified, & then we have the tools to solve these technical questions. This means that the essential questions, the questions that we should actually be asking about our school, are not being asked at all. For example, it is almost a proverb, a slogan, a catchphrase:

"Johnny can't read." Our kid can't read. Now a computer company comes along, in this case IBM, & presents a computer system, together with the program *Learning to read* & says, there we have it. & it turns out in experiments that this program, this system, actually helps to improve the reading data. Now you say:

'You see, the computer is the solution to this problem.' What you didn't do but should do is ask him why Johnny can't read. So that you can see that this is a very serious problem in our country: Officially, that is, announced by the government, we know that a third of our young people cannot read. A third of our young people! That means they can read comic *books to* some extent & also read signs, but they might not even read the tabloid here, & they especially can

Do not read the instructions for use of simple instruments. But the question should not be:

"Do we have an instrument that might help with learning to read?" It's more apt to ask, "Why can't Johnny read? Why can't he learn to read at school?' If you asked that question, it might turn out - it's just an example - that Johnny was hungry when he was in class. & if that's the case, then the next question comes up: »We always had a breakfast & lunch program at school. So, he's going to be fed, isn't he?' The answer to that is, 'No, we had it, yes sure, but we don't have it anymore.' Then the question arises, 'How come we don't have it anymore?'

"Because we don't have the money."

"Where's the money?"

Then you should know that an Air Force bomber costs - it's almost unbelievable - 700 million dollars. Without spare parts. Just the plane. 700 million dollars. You can imagine the cost of an aircraft carrier & the whole fleet that goes with it. We have a great many of these things, & they also cost something to use. It costs a lot of money. That's where the money from the lunch program went, among other things. So if you follow the question of why »Johnnycan'tread«, then you come pretty soon, I would say almost immediately, to political questions. Political questions that aren't very pleasant. Of course, the computer is not to blame for these developments, but it is used to suppress the essential questions.

Incidentally, it turns out that the children in America are not only unable to learn to read because they are hungry. There are many reasons. One of the main reasons is that children & teachers are afraid when they are at school

are. Not long ago, the drug problem was the biggest, worst problem in our school system. Now it's not. Why not? Not because it has been dismantled & diminished, but because another problem has simply increased, & that is the problem of guns in schools. So you can imagine that children & teachers are pretty scared. In the city of Detroit, Michigan - a city perhaps the size of Hamburg - about 70 children are murdered at school by other children every year. & Detroit isn't the worst city in that regard. One can imagine that teachers & children are scared. In such an atmosphere it will certainly be difficult to teach anything, whether that is reading or something else.

A third reason is that a large number of America's children - it is often said that it is a third of our children - live in poverty. Such a large number of our children in America live without hope & they simply cannot see why they should read or learn anything else. It wouldn't do them any good, they might be the third or fourth generation in their family now, if you can even say family that never found a real job. There's just no hope & no plan to become anything. The children see the young people. & when they're told, "You can't even do a job *application* for McDonald's because you can't read well enough. Do you think you're getting anywhere?" McDonald's pays maybe five dollars an hour or a little less, & you don't really need to be able to read to work for McDonald's. They have pictures at the checkout, not numbers. Then the kids might say, "But if I stand guard for the drug dealer on the corner, I get $500 a day." So how do you convince the kids that learning to read is vẹry important?

So, thẹ quality of a school systẹm is a mattẹr of prioritiẹs, & I would say that thẹ primary purposẹ of a school must bẹ to hẹlp studẹnts mastẹr thẹir own languagẹ, to bẹ ablẹ to rẹad & writẹ & spẹak clẹarly. Wẹ can't do that in Amẹrica.

Now to thẹ quẹstion that must bẹ on your mind:

"What is thẹ school's rolẹ with rẹgard to thẹ computẹr?" I would say that if thẹ school doẹs nothing at all, no computẹr classẹs, maybẹ usẹs thẹ computẹr in class, but doẹsn't tẹach computẹr sciẹncẹ, it wouldn't causẹ a catastrophẹ. I want to makẹ an analogy now. Lẹt's say instẹad of talking about thẹ computẹr at school, lẹt's talk about thẹ piano at school. & I say ẹxactly what I just said: "Yẹs, of coursẹ thẹrẹ arẹ many pianos in thẹ world, but it is not nẹcẹssary that, say, from thẹ agẹ of four you havẹ two hours of piano lẹssons ẹvẹry wẹẹk." That is not nẹcẹssary. You can also lẹarn to play thẹ piano outsidẹ of school. Thẹn somẹonẹ would ask mẹ what I havẹ against music. I havẹ nothing against music, but I don't think - this is again a quẹstion of prioritiẹs - that onẹ should havẹ thẹ attitudẹ that thẹrẹ might bẹ a young Mozart in ẹvẹry class that wẹ nẹẹd to ẹncouragẹ find thrẹẹ Mozarts.

I have nothing against the computer as such, I would like to say, nothing at all, I also have to admit that in a certain sense the computer has made a very nice life possible for me. Nor do I want to say that the computer shouldn't play a role in school. If we have children who are really interested in music, then the school should be such that the children have the opportunity to exercise their interest & learn about it. It should be the same with the computer

There should be a computer club at school, & teachers who know something about it could run the computer club & give advice. I'm pretty sure it wouldn't be long before older students could help the younger students with this, at least those who are interested.

So what then? I once asked that question to a physicist, a Nobel laureate by the way. He said: »It's very simple, every one of my students should build a computer. That's enough." Making a computer. I would say that is a reasonable answer today. It's maybe even a reasonable answer for a Waldorf school too. Maybe I should just say that everyone should have the opportunity to build a computer, that would be pretty good. Of course I don't mean now - we come back to the choice of level of explanation - that you start with electrons under stone & learn to make a very fast switch, rather that you start with these parts. Don't worry too much about the physics, but learn about the architecture of the computer. This demystifies the computer so you can see what's actually going on, & it really isn't difficult. I think something like that might do me good.

I remember my own school years. I was very fortunate to go to a public school where I had the opportunity to learn how to use lathes. At that time I had the task of building a steam engine out of very simple parts. I even had to turn these parts myself. It was a long, long time ago & I still remember. I still understand something about it, not only about steam engines but, perhaps even more importantly, about lathes

What I find particularly valuable, especially in my job, is that I have learned that the function of the lathe is not purely physical, at least not purely logical, not purely mathematical. You have your hand on a wheel that you turn & the metal bites into it. Anyone who knows it knows what I mean. You pour water over it so it doesn't get too hot, & then you spin this thing. it is also in the wrist, it is also in the arm. You learn something from it. I was very young back then & didn't think about computers at all, nobody thought about it. Now, much, much later, I'm a computer specialist, & they make computer-controlled lathes. The question arises: To what extent can one replace humans? What are the limits of artificial intelligence? What I learned there as a thirteen-year-old saved me, so to speak. I knew that you could replace people with simple jobs with a machine, but that you couldn't hand everything over to a machine. Intelligence isn't just what's going on up here in my head. With this view, I would have to break down open doors at a Waldorf school.

I also think the task of making a little computer, putting wires together & all that goes with it, means something similar. It's not quite the same, but there's something similar about it.

I am thinking of my colleague Sherry Turkle, who has written extensively about computers & children. I think her book is called Die *Wunschmaschine here;* I'm sure you're familiar with it. & I'm thinking of Seymour Papert, a colleague at MIT. If you ask him at what age you should give a child a computer for the first time, he replies that it's time when the child is born. It would soon be too late

does he mean? I'm not telling this just to tell a bad story. What he means is that you can put a child in a cradle & hang a mobile over the cradle, which is sort of computer-controlled by the computer over there. & this computer watches when the child moves. For example, the child raises its arm, just like very small babies do. & then the computer reacts to it. What is so beautiful & valuable, according to Papert, is that the child learns very, very early on that he has some control over the world. He learns that he has the opportunity to change the world. It learns that it has influence in the world, has power - that's exactly the expression that goes with it. Writing about school children,

Sherry Turkle observes that the computer gives the child - usually a boy - the first opportunity to master something completely. & for her that is the quality of the computer.

I would like to add that a skilled programmer controls a stage in the computer, so to speak, on which everything is possible. You can program a world, for example, an artificial world, where gravity, works completely differently than here, is bigger or changes, whatever. You can then throw bodies into this gravity & observe their behavior. Children, as well as adults, learn very quickly that the control you have as a programmer is absolute. Especially with modern computers, which are fairly reliable—I mean their hardware—the control is so absolute that if something doesn't work, it must be the programmer's fault. It's not like in nature that maybe something has interfered that I don't understand, or there's something there that I don't know about. No, in the case of computer simulation & the creation of artificial worlds in the computer, there can be nothing that you don't know. You put everything in yourself, assuming, of course, that you have the application book of the

computer understands. Young people can do that. Of course, it's a big attraction that kids who haven't experienced anything but helplessness are finally getting something they can handle.

But one should ask: Isn't that the technical solution to a problem that doesn't have its origins in technical questions at all? Aren't the essential questions that affect children suppressed in the process? One should rather ask how the world of the children, whether in the family or at school or elsewhere, can be designed in such a way that the children can perceive themselves as participants in the current world instead of as mere spectators or even as victims. The environment of the children & our environment in general plays a very important role. The world in which most children live today is a world that is becoming more & more abstract, which is more & more abstract. It is a world that they experience on the screen instead of in the actuality of their environment.

I suppose in families that send their children to Waldorf schools it is important to care for living beings. Maybe they have a garden & a pet. Perhaps their children are responsible for a bunny's life, not just for the next hour, but for the whole thing, instead of watching nature & wildlife movies on TV about exotic creatures to admire. & of course it's not just animals & plants that we get to know through television & not in concrete terms. The world is becoming more & more abstract, we don't experience large parts of the world in concrete terms.

It is often said that children today know much more than we knew when we were their age. I remember as a kid I thought the city of Honolulu was an invention. That's such a beautiful name, I couldn't believe a city like that actually existed

don't make mistakes They know full well there's Honolulu, they've seen it a thousand times on television about police & violence & detectives & helicopters. They know Honolulu. But what they lack is personal experience.

When you see on TV how sharks are hunted or how a spider can live under water, you have no responsibility for these living beings that you "get to know." You just see them, they are there. But when you have a rabbit or a bird or a dog to care for, you have a responsibility. & also - this is a very important point I want to emphasize - mastering a computer is irresponsible. You created this world in the computer yourself, or it was created by another computer programmer. I'm thinking here in particular of the many computer games that exist in the world. I mean the many military or quasi-military computer games that exist where, for example, children, mostly boys, sit & press a button very frantically. With every push of a button, a spaceship is shot down or a city destroyed. We have a game like that in America where you get points for how many Indians you shoot in a certain amount of time & such atrocities. There's even a game where you're the commander of a concentration camp, & many military games where you shoot down airplanes, destroy cities, etc. What do you learn from that? Above all, one learns to separate one's own activities, what one does oneself, from the consequences of one's actions. You learn that you don't have to take responsibility for the things you do. We think so - & now I come to my university

– In a technical university where good people, who are very good to their children, research & manufacture technologies that will undoubtedly be incorporated into mass murder machines such as cruise missiles. Everyone

Advances in this area are immediately built into such instruments. & they don't understand that they are responsible for it. What they do & what becomes of it is absolutely separate for them. I think we should defend ourselves against that.

Another problem I once wrote about is possible addictive behavior. There are compulsive programmers. Fortunately, they are the exception. What is interesting is that all compulsive programmers are men. Women do not seem to be prone to this addiction. That's very interesting. I'm amazed that no behavioral scientist has taken this up & tried to explain why this is so. I would like to add that this compulsive programming is just *a special case* of a much more general addiction found among scientists. The programmer in particular is able to create a world that he can completely control. I already mentioned that. This creates something of a battle between the programmer & the machine. The programmer decides something, & it is very rare that a program will actually do what the programmer intended to do on the first try, especially in the case of a very complex system. When the computer does something that is not intended - I'll just call it a "bug" - the programmer, especially the compulsive one, knows full well exactly that it's his fault.

Therefore there is a constant competition, a game between the programmer & the machine. The machine keeps showing him that he can't control it, but he wants to control it. That's why he soon doesn't do anything else *but* program

eventually has all their money & therefore

the game has to stop, then he will lend them money to continue the game. Then he ends up playing against himself. This is very stupid. The fight is the important thing! The programmer is also always moving forward: when he has built a large system & when it works, he is in a similar situation as the player. Most of the time, he'll make a small change to make it better. In trying to make it a little better, he destroys the whole thing, & then it starts all over again. What is behind it is a striving for power. I believe that is also the case with many natural scientists & also with engineers. However, the analogy with compulsive gamblers is not congruent. I am happy to say that there is one big difference: the compulsive gambler is very rarely cured & usually gambles a lifetime. But the compulsive programmer gives up after ten or twenty years of experience. It may be that he has finally gotten bored & no longer enjoys it.

school: In connection with school & computers, the question of the quality of *educational software, school software*, often arises. I mean, if the *educational software, the school software*, is bad, then we should ask why that is. It will turn out that there are serious societal reasons leading to this & that it has nothing to do with the fact that teenagers or even children do not learn very much about computers at school. I was once asked if I thought it was possible to produce reasonable school software, & my answer was: The question is whether it is possible to establish a school system in which computer software can be used reasonably .

I have already mentioned the idea that many have of technology as a cure, not a panacea but a cure. One way to question that is for students to build their own computers. That demystifies quite a lot. But you have to expand the context, it's not the technology that's breaking through here, it's the insane applications, & they have to do with the character of our society. Not only in the military, but we unnecessarily complicate our lives by introducing technology where it's unnecessary, maybe even nonsense. I'm thinking right now about things like a bathroom where there aren't faucets that you turn on & off, you just run your hands over the sink holes. Then there is a computer system that senses that my hands are there & the water runs. Something like that is absolutely unnecessary.

I once had to walk a very long time in Zurich because I had no change for the ticket machine. The machine was there, but I had no change & there was no one to beg for. If you calculate how much it costs to pay all the machines & inspectors for the subway, the S-Bahn or the tram, you might come up with a sum that would lead to the realization that it would be better if this public transport were simply free .I think it might be cheaper to do it for free than with all those tickets & machines & what that entails. I won't say it is, but it could be. But what I do know for sure is that we should be looking for social inventions.

I want to tell you a little story, a fantasy I had, not a nice one. I think so

Concentration camps in which everything that can be decided by machines - a computer is such a machine - i.e. who dies tomorrow & who stands guard is decided by a computer. In this fantasy I see two prisoners & one says to the other: It must be possible to use a computer in a sensible & humane way. & the other answers: Yes, but not in a concentration camp. I don't want to claim that we live in a concentration camp in the western world in the industrialized countries today, but I do claim, & I will also defend it, that we live in a madhouse. There are places of sanity in it, & those who live in & create such a place should strive to increase these places in the hope that the world can be saved after all. What I mean to say is that the fear we have of technology has to do with the structure of our world. I do not mean that the task is that everyone must become a revolutionary or that we should all take to the streets or to the barricades. However, we should have an awareness of where the reasons lie & what the actual problem is, rather than always just looking at the external factors & tinkering with them. I believe this is very necessary.

What should we do? I can't answer that for anyone else, everyone has to decide for themselves. In any case, don't do anything stupid! Especially when we know we're doing something stupid.

Let's take pollution as an example. We know for sure. But whether we have the will to organize politically to actually change something is another question. Right now, the industry is asking for more research into the greenhouse effect, & cigarette companies in America are still claiming that it's not scientifically proven that cigarettes make people sick

It hasn't been scientifically proven yet, we should do more experiments - such nonsense, we know it very well. & we also know exactly what we have to do, for example to keep the environment clean, & I think we know what we have to do in many other areas, but we still ask each other: What can we do? I think the question itself is very often an evasion. It means I know what I need to do, but maybe there's something that's a little easier & still allows me to do what I've bęcomę accustomęd to in this lifę.

Art & Computęr

I think thę basic motivation of thę artist is that hę has somęthing to say. Thę artist has somęthing to say, it urgęs him to say somęthing, & it's somęthing unsayablę. This is thę difficulty out of which art arisęs. Thę artist usęs his tools to transcęnd thę boundarięs of ordinary languagę. Whęn I say languagę now, I don't męan Ęnglish & Gęrman, i.ę. thę usual human languagęs, but I also męan mathęmatics. Thę artist wants to say somęthing that cannot bę said in ordinary languagę. & to gęt around what's pushing him, hę trięs to push thę boundarięs of ordinary languagę with his tools; that is, to bręak thę boundarięs. & that is an attęmpt that is bound to fail. It doęsn't work.

To put it a littlę diffęręntly, first on thę subjęct of what

"unspęakablę" is: I insist - it is a basic attitudę - that wę know much morę than wę can say. Wę all. & now, whęn I say "can say," I ręally męan in any languagę or symbol systęm, math, or chęmical notation, or music, whatęvęr.

Wę know a gręat dęal that wę cannot say. I would ęvęn say that most of what wę know is unspeakable.

»One can express a lot with words, just not the living truth«, Eugène Ionesco once said.

I would now like to turn to artificial intelligence. This theme of what is "sayable" & what is "unsayable" also plays a role there.

If I say that we know more than we can say, then the students in universities like

Stanford or MIT, who are very enthusiastic about artificial intelligence & who believe that man is nothing more than a machine, an example & then think they have me. We may not be able to say it, but we can talk about it.

For example, I suppose everyone has had the experience of having a dream so beautiful that when you wake up you try to go back to sleep in order to continue dreaming the dream. That doesn't work very long. You can't fall asleep again & again. So you try to keep the dream somehow different. There are several methods that one might use. One is to write down the dream. Another is to tell someone the dream. The third method is to tell it to yourself. In his own language, so to speak. It turns out that any method used here destroys the dream. Unfortunately, that's the way it is.

If you really want to keep the dream, there is nothing else to do but let it go. You know something here that you can't tell. This is an example. There are, of course, many, many others. & for this very reason, attempts to teach computers artificial intelligence are doomed to failure.

Back to art: to make art, the artist must master the tools of an instrument, whatever that is. One of my daughters wanted to take piano lessons & she was very impatient. There are these scales that you have to play over & over again, these finger exercises, & it gets boring very quickly. There's the teacher, & you have to practice & practice until you finally internalize it, until you get to a stage where you're no longer attached to techniquethinks, but just can do it.

We experience many things in our everyday life that require something similar, e.g. For example, writing by hand or even using a typewriter or driving a car. These are activities that we first have to become aware of. Then we slowly internalize them & stop thinking about them. Now we can write beautifully or drive well or even play the guitar.

Now I speak of the instruments. It is clear that the poet does not only have the typewriter or the pencil as an instrument. There are also arts of language that reside in him almost unconsciously, that he has internalized. It's the same with other instruments. I think it's nonsense to ask whether art is possible or impossible with certain instruments. It is also nonsensical to assume that certain instruments inevitably produce art.

The artist, who we assume is creative, can take a new object, a stone or a computer, & say that it could be an instrument of art. Now I dropped the word computer. I don't think the question of whether you can make art with a computer is a particularly good question, because it doesn't depend on the computer, it depends on the people, on the artist himself. Not long ago I saw an artist making large sculptures out of garbage, things he finds on the street & on the beach. What is emerging is beautiful, the way I see it. & I suppose that for him, if he is satisfied with that, it expresses something which he cannot otherwise say in a certain sense. & the question, can you make art with rubbish, is, as I said, not a good question.

But now we come to the computer & I hope you all know that you can do a lot of nonsense with the computer in the name of art or in the name of something else

agree when I say that maybe most, or at least a large part, of what you see at events like Ars Electronica is trivial & shouldn't be called art. If I take a brush & oil paint & paint something somewhere, the fact that I've used an artist's tools doesn't mean I've made art. So when someone uses the computer to represent something, it's not obvious that it has to be art. That's very different from saying you can't make art with a computer. The computer is an instrument – & it is so often said »a tool« (I have much more to say about that, but not here) – with which one can also make art.

I mentioned the poet & we know there are today

"Poems" produced *by a computer (Computer Generated Poetry).* I'm thinking of one of my colleagues who is world famous: Seymour Papert. He thinks a lot about computers & children & has written a famous book: *Mind Storms.* I don't know if it was translated into German. Talks about Computer Generated *Poetry* & that children can write such a program that makes it possible. I have a serious question about this, & it is: In my opinion, a poem is the poet's attempt to express something that simple words cannot say. He needs the poem to express it. Ultimately, this means that the poem represents an idea. Someone has an idea & wants to present it, & a poem is the appropriate representation they find for it. & now I ask myself, where did the idea for *Computer Generated Poetry come from?* Is there an idea in the computer? I'd say if you can't say the computer had an idea then you really shouldn't call it a poem. & I think it's kind of an insult to the poet to suggest that the

computer that has the ability to write poetry.

My position is that *Computer Generated Poetry* is nonsense. You might say: you've done different experiments, you've taken poems that were written by humans & others that the computer "wrote," & it turns out most humans can't tell the difference. If that's a contradiction, does that mean the computer can make art? My answer is, not at all.

Another example of the problem of defining art. You go for a walk on the beach & you find a nice piece of wood, you take it home, you frame it or put it up somewhere, & that's called *found art* . Whose art is that? This is where, I think, we really come to the question: Who made the art, whose art is it, what is art anyway? There are libraries full of answers to these questions, there are treatises upon treatises. What I want to say about it is quite simply that art in this context is a kind of selection. You see a piece of wood & think it's beautiful, & there are thousands of other pieces of wood on this beach & you don't take them. The person who made this selection is the artist. He made the art.

It is the same with the poet. He chose

these words, this rhythm. That's the art. It may well be that when I read a poem by a certain poet, I cannot understand why people find it beautiful & call it art. That has to do with me & with the fact that I just don't have enough practice or insight to recognize something like that. So if *ComputerGeneratedPoetry* is looked at here & someone says it's beautiful, a person certainly did it, then he saw the beauty, then hater made the selection & not the computer.

The programmer has chosen the rules according to which the computer writes. Whether the programmer deserves praise for having chosen these editing rules, I don't know. That depends on how much the praise is worth, I would think. In any case, he shouldn't say the computer writes poetry. It's not just about poems for me, it can also be essays. There are experiments here in which the system uses grammatical rules & can classify words by noun, compound adjective. You can then give the computer words from any vocabulary & it will start. What is now being published is in fact language. Grammar & sentence structure are correct. But I wouldn't say that the computer had a good idea about it.

I'll start this time with the end of my

presentation. At the end of my presentation the question is, & I'm pretty sure that the question will also be asked here: yes, but what should we do then? What do you advise us? I mean now as a result of the things I'm going to say here. So what should we do? & I'm going to give you my answer right now, it's just my answer, it's not *the* answer, there isn't. I want to word it carefully, that's why I've written it here. You should begin to show the madness to the people with more & more clarity & clarity.

What madness am I talking about when I speak of the madness of our world? What madness am I talking about then? I hope everyone here remembers the movie *The Bridge on the River Kwai.* I think the film is much more important than people thought when it first came out. I only remember one scene at the end of the film - the bridge is already built - which shows the Colonel again - it was Alec Guinness - walking up & down that bridge like only either an English Colonel or Alec Guinness can walk. & he's got a staff like the ones the English officers carry under his arm. He walks up & down, looks at the work, his work, it is wonderfully made. He is a trained civil engineer himself. Suddenly he sees a stain. He takes his staff & uses it to wipe away the stain. The bridge must be perfect. It's a bridge that he first built under duress for the Japanese in World War II, so a bridge that now benefits the enemy. Nevertheless, it had to be perfectAs I see it, dealing with the technological compulsion, so to speak, simply with the fact that the practice of natural science & technology can become a passion, one could also say an addiction. In this case it happened. You have to remember the whole movie now to know that though. As I said, he removes the stain & before him is this perfect work that he has made. Then he sees a wire down there, under the bridge, & it turns out there's a group of fighters there. One of them used to be a prisoner in that Japanese prison camp. Now he's come back with dynamite & he's going to blow up the bridge. Everything is about to explode. After the colonel has discovered the wire, a small battle ensues – I will now make it very brief. There are maybe ten or twenty people involved shooting at each other. Then one sees one who was already wounded up on the bank. He watches the whole scene & he says one word, he says madness. Just the word *madness* in English. He said that word maybe twice. I think that's one of the most important parts of this movie. & I think it's a commentary on our world. I think we live in a madhouse, our world is insane.

Whatever the Gulf War showed us in terms of technology & computers, arms trade, trade in scientific knowledge, technological innovations, knowledge of how to make toxic gas, how to keep improving missile technology; this is just insane. This whole arms trade, back & forth all over the world, is definitely not only involved in Germany, there is the Soviet Union, there is America, there is France, there is Switzerland & many other countries. It's just madness.

What I mean to say is that this man sitting there on the shore

& looks at it, maybe for the first time in his life realizing quite clearly that this is madness & speaking it out. That's what I recommend you do, or let's say I ask you to do it. I've seen some shorts here, or parts of shorts, that do exactly that & I'm delighted.

There's also some of the madness that I'm very familiar with because it's a big part of my world -- I mean the world of the university, specifically the Massachusetts Institute of Technology .Especially the computer department, i.e. the *Computer Science Department* –

"Computer science," as they call it here. This department is very, very closely linked to the Pentagon, & most closely related to artificial intelligence research, & especially to research in *visionresearch*. Therewillat

"Seeing machines" have been worked on so that computer-controlled devices, robots & cruise missiles, can see even better & hit things even better than they can today. & of course that's madness too.

Here I would like to state that without the work of scientists, without our even enthusiastic cooperation in such things, modern warfare would not be possible at all. The war will not take place without us. That's why we, as computer scientists, have little right to say that other people, for example, will accuse the politicians of what they are doing there. It wouldn't work without us. We have it in our hands, we computer scientists, I think, to almost abolish war, but that's something else, anyway it's madness too. Part of that madness is the joy we all experience, I mean

now all engineers & all scientists, maybe even all scientists, but scientists anyway, the joy we experience when we can make something very sophisticated work. That's great fun. I don't know if the public understands, "theme non-the street," so to speak, the huge role that fun plays in science, technology, engineering, & all that. If they understand what a huge motivation that is. What a joy it is when you think up a nice neat trick, when you try to implement it, make the device, write the program, & when you start to say it you could almost say live. It's a lot of fun.

For example, I'm thinking of a piece of

work that was done in what's called the Medialab at MIT that appears in a little movie here. I don't know which of you saw this film. Anyway, there's talk of a *warroom, a war* room, where someone sits in a big chair, looks at a screen & gives orders. Gives the command that the map of the Caribbean should now appear. He says that to the system. Then you see the map, the islands, Cuba, etc. On the sea you see different ships, & then he points to one & says, "Put that there." He only issues this command with his voice. Of course, the question immediately arises as to how the system understands

"that", "put that there"? The ship is to be moved, yes, points his eyes at it, first looks this way & then that way. "Putthatthere."

In another film that I also saw here, you see a pilot who looks back & forth with his eyes, & something in the plane is modified by it, so to speak. There is a device that watches his eyes & uses them to get information. All of this was developed at MIT. "Put that there. Put it back where it was." A computer scientist who knows these applications knows how difficult these problems are. What does "where it was" mean? Does it mean last time or yesterday or last year or what? & it's just a lot of fun to get such a system going. However, we must recognize that such applications will ultimately be used in the military, for example in the Gulf War.

I would like to give two more examples of the relationship between research at MIT & the military. About six months ago there was a conference in Hamburg. A scientist I didn't know personally, who apparently worked in the Medialab at MIT, had given a lecture on art & computers. It was a very nice lecture with many slides, very colorful, in beautiful colors. I assume that many here know the story of *The Little Prince* of Saint-Exupéry; his lecture had to do with this story. You see a beautiful picture on the screen, the background is so deep blue, you see small dots, they are stars, & then somewhere down there you see something that looks like a tennis ball. So, all yellow against this blue, & that is a planet. On the planet you can see various flowers, palm trees, there is also a volcano, etc. Somewhere there is a smiling girl, a small child, & there is a clown somewhere up there

— yes, what is done with these things? A device is being developed that can, so to speak, calculate where the eyes of an observer are directed. With the help of this device, which is now watching over the observer, well, with this

instrumentyou can see where he is looking & where he is looking most. You can also make statistics about what interests you & what doesn't. It's all very sophisticated, there must be a lot of computers behind the scenes. The scientist explained all this & showed various examples, including statistics that can calculate it all. Then we suddenly no longer see fairy tale images as an example, but a satellite image of an airport, a military airport with planes, armored vehicles, but also a parking lot with cars. The task now is, among other things, to recognize what things are involved. The computer system that has this picture in front of it should recognize what is an airplane, what is a tank, what is a car. This is yet another example of trying to hide technological military developments behind a fairy tale. We paint such beautiful pictures in such bright colors & it's all so beautifully sweet, but actually it's about teaching the computer, especially the military computer, to see & use this technology to support applications like the Gulf War. Well, I want to emphasize that we're telling each other fairy tales. The fairy tale we told each other last is very well known: it is the fairy tale of the clean war.

Another project is the so-called *Autonomous Vehicle System*. This system must recognize whether a moving vehicle is a tank or a tank or who knows what, & then decide whether to destroy it or not. The name for this device is *Autonomous Land*

Vehicle, which means it is autonomous, there are no people around. With the help of artificial intelligence, this vehicle is sent out & then has to decide who to shoot & who not to shoot.

The question arises to me: why do we need such things or why does the military need such things at all? & a second one

Question that comes to my mind is: how do we learn to put aside our conscience so successfully? So why do we need, why does the military need things like this?

The first thing to say about this is that the increasing speed of our technological systems is now forcing us to produce systems at even greater speeds. It's a vicious circle, of course, it's just going on, it's a spiral. In the beginning - the computer isn't that very, very old, I'm talking about the early 1950's now - we made an anti-bomber defense system in America, the name of which was Legend. & the signals from these large radar systems were then sent to a computer designed & manufactured at MIT. He had to analyze everything & warn when Russian planes were coming. In the early 1950s, the threat came from planes, not from rockets. Why was this done? Because the reaction time that a person would have if he himself looks at the radar screen would be too long. It had to be analyzed by the computer. In this area, everything has become so fast that one person alone could no longer do it without this technical help. Today, of course, everything has become much, much faster.

Then came the *ballistic missiles,* I want to emphasize *ballistic now* , which means they have to go up somewhere, have to fly through the stratosphere & then the upper stratosphere & then come back into the stratosphere & so on. It takes a long time, they are launched from a *great* distance Soviet Union is shot down before it lands in Chicago. That's maybe twenty minutes or twenty-five even, & that's a very long time now. Today, of course, are

times much shorter. To make everything faster, humans had to be eliminated as much as possible. The computers we had back then weren't fast enough, so we had to have faster computers. Then it also became possible that such weapons - if one may call such instruments weapons - could be parked in space, perhaps in the last parking lot in the whole world. They were deployed as satellites & could then be unleashed when the enemy - whoever that is - decided that we should be killed. Worse, now we have missiles on submarines that can be launched near shore, & we're talking minutes & even seconds now.

Dai mentioned submarines that carry missiles: we, I mean we Americans, now have submarines that carry so many nuclear-armed *missiles* that one of these submarines could destroy the whole Soviet Union.

& I just want to point out that the name of one of these submarines is - I can hardly *pronounce it - Corpus Christi. You have* to realize that someone made it up. That didn't come from the computer; a person thought about it.

Within the military technical systems, the human being is of course the weakest link, or at least is regarded as such. The weakest link must then of course be further & further pushed aside, pushed out. In recent times we have experienced various adventures in which one person ultimately had to decide. I think of the Airbus that was shot down over Iran. In the end, someone had to decide whether to do it or not, & there simply wasn't time for careful consideration. The response to this incident isn't to stop this shooting, which might be sensible, but to just squeeze the man, in this case the commander, out

thissystem.Itshouldbecomefullyautomatic.

That brings us -- that's nice logic -- to the *Autonomous Land Vehicle* I mentioned earlier. It makes all the decisions on its own, no one is there. One could say that the computer with its artificial intelligence is now responsible, but of course the question arises: What can it mean that a computer is responsible? In any case, that has the additional advantage, as we also heard in the Gulf War, that our soldiers are then less endangered. The other soldiers might be endangered, but maybe they also have *Autonomous LandVehicles,* I don't know

– & I think it is very important – is the lesson of different video games.

So how are the various video games related to the Gulf War? It has been remarked many times that the Gulf War as we perceived it looked a lot like a video game. The lesson of the video game is that the psychological distance of the consequences of an act from the act itself is magnified astronomically. This means that the child who plays video games, does it as fast as possible in order to collect points & win the game. The fact, i.e. what is symbolized in the game, e.g you shoot down a plane & it burns & the pilot dies in it - that's astronomically far from the child's consciousness. It also has to be so far away, otherwise you wouldn't be able to press the button so quickly. When President Reagan was at an EXPO in Florida a few years ago & he was shown how the boys play computer games like this, he proudly said: These are our fighter pilots of the future! He was absolutely right

professions in this insane world is very appropriate. Above all, that means that the psychological distance, the distance between what I do & what the consequences of my action are, is so huge that these two things simply have nothing to do with each other anymore. We saw that in the Gulf War. We saw - you've heard it a thousand times, I'll say it again very briefly - the beautiful electronics & then such an explosion, purely symbolic, without people there. We didn't see the corpses, the ripped off heads, arms & legs that you see in war - quite unlike the Vietnam War where we did see those things. President George Bush said very often: This is not Vietnam! & I think he meant this too: This time we will see such pictures, no blood, no red colors at all. That allows - I don't know if I can put it that way - the world public, at least the American public, to simply cheer for what is being done, & especially for what technology, our technology, has done & can do War. I'm not going to say the video games are to blame, that's nonsense, of course, but they taught us a lot & prepared us well.

I'd like to say a word about the phrase "clean gulf war." There is a repression involved again, not just the ones I just mentioned. I mean this: There is a profession or subject in *America* called humanization of work. In this context, I have a fantasy: Some people from the field *of humanization of work* visit a factory somewhere. The factory is dark, it is hot inside & very dusty,

the workers work far too close together & the machines are not secured at all. You can hurt yourself on these machines. The sanitary facilities are awful & far away & there is a tremendous amount of noise in the room. Then they do their work, & maybe half a year later you look at this factory again. It's bright now, good air, the machines are far apart & all secured, you can't hurt yourself there, you could do surgery in the toilets, they're so clean & it's very quiet, maybe you can even hear a little music in the background . Now you realize: That is humanization of work. But you should also ask what is done in this factory? & if it turns out that this factory makes furnaces in which people are cremated, you should say: we shouldn't humanize that, we should get rid of that.

I believe there is a close connection between the clean Gulf War & this fantasy of humanizing work. We see this war as if through a telescope & not in a wide angle, but in a very narrow angle. We only see details. We see – & that's shown to us so nicely on television – how this rocket is steered to the Baghdad water works & how it hits it there exactly. It hits a very specific door, destroys everything, & apart from the two or three people who might happen to be working there, nobody gets hurt - & that's clean. It's very different from what happens when B52s drop thousands of bombs. & if we look a little wide-angle, just like at this factory, & ask ourselves what they're actually doing there, then we see something that's not so clean anymore: If you destroy the water works of a big city, the risk of epidemics increases for the entire population.

The war is very dirty & it is a lie to say that no civilians are being killed. I advocate this wide *angle view* of what we are doing & hope we do not soon forget the example of the Gulf War.

A word about forgetting in general: President George Bush has said many times over the past few weeks that the Vietnam trauma, the Vietnam Syndrome, is now behind us. It shouldn't be behind us & the gulf war should never be behind us, we must remember that! We need to know what we can do & have done. Bush invites repression. That's bad, we shouldn't repress.

Before I wrap up, I want to address two things: the perceived helplessness & my personal work at MIT.

Regarding supposed helplessness, I would like to say that above all we who have this opportunity, I as a teacher & you as a filmmaker, must not say that we are helpless. You can just – easy?! - don't let it be misused! You have to think – I speak the same way to computer scientists – you have to think about what you're actually doing. & as a filmmaker - I'm not from your field, but the way I see it from the outside - you also have to ask yourself: Am I being abused? Do I let myself be abused? Is it possible for me to tell the truth in my work as I see it? I know there are many different versions of truth, but we may be the very last who have this opportunity to speak to many people & in a language that transcends the usual boundaries of language. By that I mean film, music & art. that they are helpless, then everything is over. The Stalins of this world, the Hitlers of this world, they know that. That's why they exterminate their artists.

I don't want to leave unanswered the important question of how I personally dealt with the madness of the military, the question & problem of why & how I worked as a critic at MIT & what my position there was. You might imagine that it is very difficult for me personally at MIT, but it is not at all. I have often had the fantasy of teaching at a college or university that is quite liberal, out in the country with forest & meadows around. I imagined a small university with liberal, even progressive, students & staff. There are universities like that in America too. But I'm quite sure that if I were in a university like that, I would wish I was at MIT. How I am treated there is another matter. It's perfectly clear to me that the administration uses me & maybe others as a fig leaf. When people complain about blind faith in technology or ask whether there aren't any critical voices about computers at MIT, then they say: Yes, Professor Weidenbaum, he thinks about such things & writes about them. My relationship, my relationship with my colleagues is a bit more complicated. who is critical of his subject. The most famous name I can give you right away is Noam Chomsky. Second, unfortunately, I have often had a certain experience: when I speak—whether it is in a *faculty meeting* or in front of a class or at a demonstration—some of my colleagues come up to me later, put their arm around my shoulder & say, "You said that well, that needs to be said. I'm glad you said it.' They may also say very quietly to themselves: Now that it's been said, it doesn't need to be said anymore. That could be the case. I'm sad that so many of my colleagues support me privately, but just

145

never to them
go public.

We invented weapons & weapon systems for the Vietnam War at MIT, so I can tell long stories, cruel stuff. MIT is very closely connected to the Pentagon. & then, as a Jewish German emigrant in America, I had to ask myself whether I now want to play the role that I hated so much with many, even most German scientists, professors, academics, here in Germany during the Hitler era. This attitude of saying: I'm a scientist, that's my field, & what is done with my thing is none of my business. I'm not a politician. Other people are responsible for that. I am also thinking here of Wernher von Braun, who wrote a book: / *aimed for the stars, & I invented a* subtitle for it »... but sometimes I hit London«. When asked about the goals of his research, his answer was:

"That's not my department."

During the time of the Vietnam War & during the time of the civil liberation movement in America, I asked myself whether I wanted to play the role of these German professors or not.

Today I'm retired & I still have my office at MIT. I also had my last graduate student until recently. I can give lectures if I want, well, I'm still not far from MIT today. I'm still here. It's become clear to me that MIT was my placę & that I bęlong therę. Pęrhaps it's also bęcausę of my arrogancę that I thought MIT's studęnts & young collęaguęs nęędęd my voicę morę than anywhęrę ęlsę. That's why I stayęd.

I męntionęd Noam Chomsky ęarlięr. Noam Chomsky, thę linguist, is onę of thę gręatęst gęniusęs of this cęntury,

I am convincęd of that. I assumę a lot of pęoplę hęrę know him, I hopę so anyway. Hę's bęęn tęaching at MIT for, I think, thirty-fivę yęars. Hę's ręcęivęd ęvęry honor MIT can bęstow, as węll as many intęrnational awards. During thę timę of thę Viętnam War, whęn hę was a lęading voicę in thę ręsistancę against this war - hę protęstęd loudly & wrotę a lot about it - I somętimęs spokę to studęnts & said Noam Chomsky would do it or Noam Chomsky would say that ętc. Thęy answęręd yęs, that's Noam Chomsky, hę can do it. Hę can afford it, hę hę's such a big guy. Thęn I had to say, but hę wasn't always thę gręat Noam Chomsky. Hę was oncę a bęginnęr, *assistant profęssor,* & ęvęn thęn - & I must ęmphasizę this - in thę first post-war yęars at MIT as a vęry minor *assistant* profęssor with no guarantęę of any futurę othęr than thę onę hę had in mind, ęvęn thęn hę insistęd that ęvęryonę knows hę is an anarchist. Hę is an anarchist, a committęd anarchist. All his lifę, in thę academy & outside, he acted as an anarchist & never denied it. Nothing happened to him. & not because he was big, he was small then. Noam Chomsky never hid his political stance at all, even when he was a little *assistant* professor, very fragile, so to speak, very vulnerable, so he already had a critical attitude.

Now I'm getting back to the question I started with. I'm addressing the filmmakers among you now. You can ask, yes, but what are we supposed to do? I mean very specifically with the technical means that come from the MIT laboratory, i.e. that are actually intended for the military, although you can also use them to take beautiful pictures for *civil life* . What should we do with it? I've already given the answer, I'll just do it.repeat: I would say you should stop gorging on the poisoned fruits of madness. Full of food – I wrote that on my note here in memory of Brecht. I really mean – I know it's very difficult to implement – you should refrain from these sophisticated things, you should simply say: No, that's blood, it was made for other purposes that we don't want anything to do with anymore. That supports the madness of this world, & we don't do that. I recommend that. You should start, or those of you who are already doing it, should continue to show people more & more clearly, with more & more clarity, the madness that is in our world.

The Responsibility of Scientists & Possible Limits

Can a restriction of research be equated with censorship of natural science? Censorship is a harsh word, & yet I would say: »Yes, but there is no other way.« But then we should also address the question of where the restrictions on research should come from. The word "should" refers to a quality of thinking that is not exactly scientific. A fundamental limitation of research, whether we like it or not, is time. Time a mortal has to create something. There is an infinite amount of work to do & only finite resources. The human talent resource in particular is limited. In principle, there are an infinite number of questions that scientists can ask, but for a generation or two there are very few questions that can actually be asked. This means that each generation must choose which questions to answer & which not to. We have to leave some questions to our children – the next generation. & there may also be questions that we shouldn't answer at all.

Are there ideas that shouldn't be thought of? I don't believe that thinking can be forbidden. But what about the ideas? The following joke is told by Albert Einstein: A young journalist interviews Einstein & asks him if he always carries a small notebook with him. Einstein doesn't understand the question & says:

"No, why?" The journalist says, "Well, just in case

that you have an idea." Einstein replied, "You know, young man, in my whole life I've only had two or three ideas."

So we couldn't really forbid the development of ideas, it's not possible. But maybe there are ideas that come to mind that we shouldn't pursue any further. At the very least, we should ask ourselves why these ideas emerged. A psychiatrist once told me: We can't help falling in love, but we can decide what we do then. In the same way, we can also decide what to do with ideas. We should be aware that the world is not a private testing laboratory for scientists. That scientists have responsibilities.

E.g. gene manipulation: People can dream up all sorts of things, but once they start doing experiments, they can't decide on their own that the whole environment should become their private testing lab. So there are limits, & there should be limits.

Are there any projects that shouldn't be done at all? Two projects can come to mind

& I'd bę amazęd if anyonę hęrę would allow them. Onę: brain opęrations on hęalthy nęwborns in thę sęrvicę of brain ręsęarch. Wę don't allow that. Why not? Whęrę doęs this inhibition comę from? & how is it donę? & thę othęr projęct: Somę collęaguęs in thę physics dępartmęnt at thę Massachusętts Institutę of Tęchnology (MIT) told mę that it would bę possiblę, in principlę, to makę an atomic bomb thę sizę of a Coca-Cola bottlę. I would say that such a projęct should simply not bę allowęd. I also don't think anyonę actually sęriously considęrs supporting such a projęct, politically, financially or through scięntific collaboration - would bę onęMisanthropę – but I don't know.

Thę idęa that thęrę arę limits to scięntific inquiry is not quitę as tęrriblę as it first appęars. In fact, wę havę cęnsorship, ęspęcially sęlf-cęnsorship. Thę quęstion is rathęr: Whęrę doęs it comę from & who is it supposęd to comę *from* ? What doęs that męan? Impęrialism is thę ęxęrcisę of powęr that doęs not lęgitimatęly bęlong to you. For ęxamplę, thę US Congręss has thę right to makę laws that allow or prohibit anything in thę US. Thę Constitution givęs Congręss that powęr. But thę US has no lęgitimatę right to dętęrminę thę form of govęrnmęnt of othęr countrięs. That is impęrialism. & by thę tęrm "instrumęntal ręason" I męan a męntality that only starts with goals to bę achięvęd or avoided. We cannot base all our actions on such reason.

Two examples: You find a wallet with a lot of money. You take it to the lost & found office so that it can be returned to the owner. Now someone comes & asks:

"Why did you do that?" It's interesting what kind of answer you're expecting now. One possible form would be to quote consequences:

'If I hadn't returned it I would certainly spend the money or put it in the bank. & then the tax authorities - in America our famous IRS *(Internal Revenue Service)* - would come & say: You have evaded tax liability. The whole thing could end very badly. That's why I gave the wallet back." The answer we expect or hope for is different: "I don't know why I gave it back. That's just how I am, that's how I was brought up.« Or: »That's how people do it here, it's so common here.« So it doesn't work

some profit

appeals to "instrumental reason" but to a different kind of reason.

A long time ago I wrote about a project proposal to artificially keep a dead cat's brain alive & use the visual field as a computer part to give the computer vision. I said that was obscene. You shouldn't do it. When I was asked why not, I gave the same answer as in the wallet example: It's disgusting, it's not decent, you just can't. One criterion is: How will the work product ultimately be used? I'm doing something, I might get a result, & I have to ask myself: What's going to happen with it? From many conversations with colleagues I know different answers to this question

– or maybe I should say: different ways of dodging the question. Eg:

"I can't know how my work will be used later." Or: "Everything can be used for good or evil, & I just hope that the application of my work is good." Or: "Where is the line between 'good' & 'bad'?" These are very difficult questions. & because one can probably not answer these questions at all, one draws the conclusion: We do not have the responsibility to make such decisions.

When it comes to computing, computing, & artificial intelligence (AI), people say, "I don't know how it will end up being used."

My answer to that: "Oh yes, you can." Here I am in a foreign country, but I can say of America that there one can very well know how the work of an AI laboratory or the laboratory in which I work, the *Laboratory for*

Computer Science, ultimately applied. In the case of MIT, we can see very clearly that if it is at all possible to somehow incorporate a research result, e.g Pentagon. You should be able to guess that this work is possibly used for military purposes. Of course, there are counter-arguments, e.g.:

"It's not my job to find out what's happening with my work." Or my old colleague in AI research at Carnegie Mellon University, Herbert Simon, with whom I had a lengthy debate on this question, who said:

"In America we have a representative form of government. We let our elected MPs decide what to do with our science. & if we don't like that, then we can choose others.«

I think that's a kind of abdication. It reminds me of the attitude of the majority of German scientists, especially during the Third Reich. We are scientists, politics is none of our business, the leader decides. What do we do with the realization that everything can be used for good & evil? Yesterday at the press conference someone said: "For God's sake, you can't ban a shoe factory just because the shoes might go to soldiers." Then comes the question: "How do you decide what is good & bad?" That is of course an age-old question, an impossible question that I cannot answer .But I can get close enough to make it easier to determine where we can draw the line, like saying, "Up to this point I'm going with it & no further."

So what is "good" & "bad" anyway? To think about it, you have to have some kind of wide-angle lens

must include a very large context. An example: If I speak as badly as is expected of me during lectures, the argument then comes: »But it must be possible to use computers for humane purposes,

eg in medicine.« When I then ask for an example, the CAT scanner is often cited, *Computer Aided Tomography*. Is there anything bad to say about the CAT scanner? As far as we know, no one has ever been killed or injured with it, but it is used to examine the living brain to determine whether surgery is necessary &, if so, where exactly the tumor is located so that surgery becomes easier.

But now in wide angle. We have to ask in which social context the CAT scanner is used. In the USA it has the effect that hundreds of thousands more people than before will never see a doctor & will not receive any medical treatment. how come American doctors work within a market economy system & are always exposed to the risk of being accused of malpractice. This means that the cost of medical treatment increases. But there is more. If I went to a doctor & said that my little finger on the right hand hurts, he would say (I'm exaggerating): We need a full check-up, so two days in the hospital, X-rays, *CAT scan,* blood tests & all sorts of extras. Why is he doing this? He doesn't want to be charged because he forgot something Medicine as such & certainly nothing with the CAT scanner. Almost every hospital has two or three CAT scanners that always need to be improved. They're very expensive, & we Americans are realizing that the healthcare system is suffering because of this technological advancesee the CAT scanner in the light of the social circumstances in which it is embedded.

With computer image recognition, it's perfectly clear - sort of determinate - that any finding that has any bearing on improving the computer's vision will be immediately picked up by the military. We can't pretend we don't know.

Assuming you don't want to further militarize the world, where do you draw the line? I think we have to draw that line partly arbitrarily. For example, we could do a poll here: everyone could write down on a little piece of paper when the day ends & when the night begins. I suppose we'll get a lot of different answers. Someone might say:

"When the sun goes down". & if you go on to ask: "Where?" - "Yes, when I'm in my apartment & the sun goes down behind that mountain..." Or an Englishman might say:

"After tea, but before the cocktail." So there are certain occasions when we decide: Here the day ends, & then the night begins. How is it done? More or less randomly. But one thing is clear: we know that noon is day, & we know that midnight is night. That is the criterion I want to apply here. So when we work to improve the aiming accuracy of a missile, it's very clear that this is "night work". I don't have to explain where to draw the line. It's just "night," that's out of the question. & there are other things that are simply "day" in the social context & that you do quietly can without feeling guilty. In this way we can make a choice between "good" & "evil," a choice that not everyone would agree with, but certainly applies to ourselves. When we have done that & ask ourselves: »How will my work be used in the end?

that into the domain 'day' or into the domain 'night'?", then we must also ask ourselves: "How far removed is this end use of my work from where I am now with it? Can it be that I am not allowed to do the work now because maybe in a hundred years it will be used for evil purposes? Or does the goal fall within the time of my own work?"

Yesterday in the press conference we talked about the responsibility of AI researchers, especially at MIT. What is the goal of AI & can we take responsibility for it? & Marvin Minsky said the goal of AI is to eliminate death. I suppose some here will be a bit surprised by that statement. But in the US it's a common idea. This discussion is already twenty years old in America, in Germany it is only now being documented. I'm thinking of the book that Marvin Minsky mentioned earlier, *MindChildren by Hans Moravec.* Moravec claims that pretty soon - unfortunately not in his lifetime, he regrets, but in those of his children - it will be possible to save a person in the computer. In English: "to download a human being into acomputer" - of course completely digitized, which means that this human being can live forever. Of course, if the computer starts to rust, then this digital information can be transferred to another computer, & then we have immortality. So it is said that the goal is the elimination of death. So why should we stop working on it? If one accepts this line of reasoning, then one is in the philosophical attitude that claims that the end justifies all means. I don't know how many barrels (that's what we would say today - we always talk about *barrels of oil),* how many barrels of blood have been spilled in the last two hundred years in the name of this philosophy.

If image recognition/AI succeeds at all, it will result in a weapon being "improved". But that knowledge is quite distant from us. We have become accustomed to creating a huge psychological distance between our actions & the effects of our actions. This is very common in our society, not only now in the last decade of this century. I think of Vietnam, of the bombing by a B52 plane flying ten thousand meters in the air. An electronic signal on a small screen tells the pilot that the target has been reached & that it is time to drop the bombs. He presses a button. The bombs fall. He can't see her. He's far away when they get down. He can't hear them. He certainly can't hear people's screams. & it's only because of that psychological distance from the effects of his actions that he's able to push that button. What I'm getting at: you do something & the consequences of your actions are repressed.

You see something similar in research labs. Here's a little story: I'm walking across Harvard Square in Cambridge, & a young man who used to be in one of my seminars approaches me. He's a graduate student now, & he wants to tell me what he's writing his dissertation on. He tells me to imagine a big screen showing a bear & a small cat. The cat throws a ball at the bear, who catches it & rolls it back towards the cat. A little girl sits in front of this screen & says to the system: "Bear, if someone gives you something, you should say 'thank you'." If the cat then throws thę ball to thę bęar again, hę says: "Thank you, dęar cat." Thęsis work is to implęmęnt this systęm. Thę pros hęrę will know that this is tręmęndously difficult work, ęspęcially whęn you want it to bę as sęamlęss as hę dęscribęd it to mę. It has to do with Sprachęr-

knowing to do & with stuff likę that. I askęd thę doctoral studęnt if hę would likę to hęar how I undęrstand thę systęm so that I can bę surę that I undęrstood it corręctly. & I tęll him this story: I sęę a pilot in thę fightęr planę & thę systęm says to him, "Sir, I sęę a column of ęnęmy tanks down thęrę." & thę pilot says to thę systęm, "If you sęę somęthing likę that, firę up thę missilęs & don't kęęp asking mę." Thęn thę rockęts go off.Pęriod.Ęnd of story. I thęn askęd thę young man if that was a dęscription of his work, & hę said yęs, you could look at it that way. & I askęd him who was paying for this ręsęarch. It turns out it was thę military. I havę had similar ęxpęrięncęs with othęr ręsęarch projęcts, which arę also dęscribęd in thę form of fairy talęs, in bęautiful colours. As an asidę, thę Pęntagon vęry raręly actually namęd a węapons systęm in its ręsęarch assignmęnts bęforę 1980, bęforę thę Ręagan administration. All sorts of ęuphęmisms węrę usęd. It wasn't until thę ęarly 1980s - *Timę Magazinę* spokę of a timę of nęw patriotism - that thę Pęntagon actually startęd calling weapon systems by their names. At MIT, three systems were being worked on, mainly in the artificial intelligence laboratory - the whole project was called SCI *(Strategy Computing Initiative). & one of the projects was* the very pilot system I described earlier: *PilotAssistance,* designed to replace the second man on the fighter plane. When we artificially create needs when many vital needs of so many people cannot be met, we create a system that eludes us. Faust did not sell his soul for free, he wanted something in return. We should ask questions & not start with the solution, also in relation to our science & technology. Astronomer Tim Peake: I am thinking of Mars flights, that is certainly very nice, but why in such a hurry?